Biographical Sketch of
Acharya Vinoba Bhave

Biographical Sketch of
Acharya Vinoba Bhave

V. Raghunathan

Raj Publications

New Delhi - 110002 (INDIA)

Biographical Sketch of Acharya Vinoba Bhave

First Published in 2006

ISBN 81-86208-47-X

The responsibility for the facts or opinions expressed is entirely of the Author and not of the Publishers.

Published by : **Poonam Goel**
Raj Publications
4855/24, Ansari Road, Daryaganj
New Delhi - 110002
Tel. : 011- 30120939, 09811010939

Laser Typesetting : Aarati Computers, Delhi-110 009

Printed at : Balaji Offset, Delhi

PRINTED IN INDIA

Preface

Vinayak Narahari Bhave, fondly known as 'Acharya Vinoba Bhave' was a great scholar, saint, man of God, moral tribune, a beacon of hope and solace to millions of Indians. He was one of the main architects of Modern India and Mahatma Gandhi's spritual successor. He played a very significant part at a crucial period in the history of the country and offered solutions to the several problems India was confronted with during the struggle for social and economical reforms.

A great innovative experimenter in Gandhian techniques, he placed reliance on the Gandhian philosophy of change of heart and used the instrument of moral appeal of the Bhoodan (donation of lands) Movement to secure land to the landless. Vinoba lead a life in accordance with the eleven vows, included in the Gandhian daily prayer viz. non-violence, truthfulness, absolute honesty, chastity, poverty, annual work, temperance, fearlessness, respect for all religions, independence in the matter of money and non-recognition of caste distinctions.

Vinoba was one of the front rank Indian nationalist leaders of India, who played a vital role in India's Freedom Struggle. He has translated his principles into practice, pressed all his philosophy and mathematics into the aid of the constructive programme which he always believed to be the external symbol of non-violence. Non-violence and compassion being a hallmark of his philosophy, he also campaigned against the slaughtering of cows.

Vinoba was more interested in land reform, accomplished voluntarily than in politics, founded the Bhoodan Movement or land-gift movement in the year 1951. The Bhoodan movement initiated by him created a social climate to land reforms and their smooth implementation. Subsequently he traveled over thousands of miles by foot, accepting donations of land for redistribution to the landless. By 1969, he collected over 4 million acres of land through Bhoodan and Gramdan for redistribution.

Vinoba's religious outlook was very broad and it synthesized the truths of many religions. This can be seen in one of his hymns "Om Tat" which contains symbols of many religions. He was also a scholar of many languages.

I am deeply indebted to Commodore Sukhjinder Singh, Judge Advocate General (Navy) and Smt. Neera Shastri, Member, National Commission for Backward Classes for their constant help, valuable guidance and encouragements. Even though the works and life of Acharya Vinoba published in the earlier writings have been an unfailing source of light and strength to human kind over the decades, it is my endeavour to bring out the complete life and works of the Acharya in a simple form in this book and I trust that the readers will find the present work equally illuminating

— V. Raghunathan

Contents

1

Early Life of Vinoba Bhave

Vinayak Narahari Bhave, fondly known as Vinoba was born at Gagoda, in the Kolaba district of Maharashtra on 11 September, 1895. Vinoba was deeply attached to his mother Rukmini Bai inherited her austerity, asceticism and altruism. His father, Narahari Shambhurao was an ardent advocate of western learning and science. Vinoba was a brilliant student. He studied Sanskrit and became proficient in all Hindu scriptural books. He was a self-taught multilinguist.

His mother was a devout lady. She knew hundreds of Marathi Bhajans and devotional songs, which she would keep on singing in the course of her domestic work. Vinoba's early character was molded mainly at the hands of his pious and affectionate mother. She led a life of simplicity and self-restraint and observed religious vows with regularity. It was at her feet that Vinoba imbibed the basic precept. 'He who gives is a God; but he who withholds is a devil.' Vinoba once told a group of workers "My mother was the source of strength. She had unlimited confidence in my capacity. That living faith of hers gave me immense strength." Vinoba's personality was shaped by the great qualities of Shambhurao Narahari and Rukminibai into an extra ordinary amalgam of the wisdom, devotion and action. Jnana, Bhakti and Karma. One comes but rarely across a man who combines the three qualities with such a distinction.

He and his three brothers – Balkrishna, Shivaji and Dattatreya spent their early childhood in the lap of nature, in the hills, forests and fields of Gagoda. They had one sister too, who was married off early, according to the then prevalent customs in rural India. Vinoba grew up in an atmosphere of discipline, loving care, revolutionary ideas and religious intensity.

It was once again his mother who encouraged Bramhacharya (celibacy) in Vinoba. From his father he got a sense of dutifulness, detachment and clear and free thinking. He also inherited from him his love of science and math. His early learning was at home in Gagoda. He learnt to read and write his mother tongue Marathi at home.

Vinoba played a most significant role in the annals of Modern India. He was a true Gandhian who came in to contact with Mahatma Gandhiji at a fairly young age. He indeed took life long pledge of celibacy and national service at the tender age of ten. He was admitted to a High School in Baroda from where he passed his Matriculation Examination. During his school days, he was an outstanding student and he never liked the oft-repeated academic courses in the educational institutions. He started the Vidyarthi Mandal at Baroda in 1914; came in to contact with Mahatma Gandhi at the Kochrab Ashram, Ahmedabad on 7th June, 1916 and met Lokamanya Bal Gangadhar Tilakji on 6th March, 1917. Vinoba was arrested at the time of Flag Satyagraha at Nagpur. He started several Ashrams at Wardha. He participated in the Civil Disobedience Movement and the Individual Satyagraha and courted imprisonment in both the occasions.

In November 1913, Vinoba passed the matriculation examination. He joined the Intermediate class of the Baroda College. But he never felt any attraction towards the modern type of education and was very critical about its real utility in life. To one of his friends, he remarked that the existing schools and colleges were only large factories for training 'your most obedient servants'. In fact he wanted to burn his boats once and for all. Vinoba wanted to sever all the connections with academic education in order to continue his quest for the eternal with single-minded devotion. He used to tell his fellow students that he was thinking of giving up his college studies to realize Brahma – *'Athato Brahmajijnasa'*. Two days before the Intermediate examination was to be held in Bombay, Vinoba boarded a Bombay-bound train at Baroda with his friend Gopalrao Kale on 25th March, 1916. He detrained at Surat and handed over a letter to Gopalrao for his father with instructions not to post it until the examinations were over. The letter ran thus "Instead of going to Bombay for taking the examination, I am proceeding somewhere else. I am sure you have trust in me that wherever I may go, I will not indulge in any unethical behaviour." From Surat, Vinoba went to Bhusaval enroute to Varanasi. His father was naturally upset when he received the letter from his son. However be believed that Vinoba would soon return home. But his mother who knew better her son remarked 'once Vinoba made up his mind, he will stick to his decision, come what may!".

At Varanasi, he started studying Sanskrit especially of the *Vedas* and the *Upanishads* at the local library in Ahilyabai Wada. He used to take simple meals from the charitable kitchens of the temples and led a very austere life. From the dakshina of two paise received from the temple, he used to purchase curd and sweet potatoes for the evening meal. After taking bath in Ganga, he used to medidate for hours. He also wrote some of the finest poems in Marathi, but offered them to the holy waters after he was satisfied with the quality of diction. In the *Gita Pravachanen*, Vinoba writes about the Ganges : When I was living in Kashi I used to go and sit on the banks of the Ganga. I would go and sit there in the loneliness of night. What beauty, what brightness in its flow! Those lovely and majestic waters and the countless stars of the sky in them! I would sit there speechless. What calm of mind was mine when my eyes were filled with the sight of the Ganga, which descended from the matted locks of Shiva, from the Himalayas, the river by whose banks Kings, casting off the symbols of power, perform their austerities. In the stillness of the peace, I began to understand why the Hindu wishes that after death his bones at least should be immersed into the Ganga. You may laugh, but that does not alter the fact." One day while returning from the Ganga, he stopped at a hardware merchant's shop to buy a lock for his small room in Durga Ghat. Vinoba selected a lock which would cost 3 annas. Taking the advantage of his innocence, the shopkeeper quoted 10 annas as its price. Vinoba promptly paid 10 annas and told the shopkeeper : "I know that this lock costs only 3 annas; but I repose trust in you and therefore give you 10 annas as asked by you. Vinoba used to pass that shop every day on his way to the river. The conscience of the shopkeeper must have been pricking him all these days. One fine day he called Vinoba and told him with repentance: "The cost of the lock was really 3 annas. Kindly take back the 7 annas and excuse me." Vinoba was deeply touched by his change.

In 1916 at the age of 20, Vinoba was in the holy city of Banaras trying to come to a decision, whether he should go to Himalayan Mountains and become a religious hermit? or should he go to West Bengal and join the movement to fight against the British? Vinoba and his friends had read in the newspapers, about a speech Gandhiji delivered on the occasion of the foundation-stone ceremony of the Banaras Hindu University at the hands of Lord Hardings, the then Viceroy of India on 4th February, 1916 which was presided over by Annie Besant, the then President of the International Theosophical Society. She had requested to Gandhiji to speak on the occasion and expected him to be so brief and to the point. However, Gandhiji bluntly criticised the display of pomp and power of the Government and took the Princess to task for their gaudy dress and costly jewellery in a poor country like India. After reading this report, Vinoba was thrilled. He was attracted towards his idea of fearlessness and non-violent resistance even into the death. Vinoba after his two months experiences in Varanasi, decided to meet Gandhiji to satisfy his political as well as spiritual urges. There was an exchange of a few letters between them. Vinoba frankly mentioned some of his doubts and difficulties and raised certain philosophical queries. Gandhiji replied that it was not possible to answer all these questions through correspondence and invited young Vinoba to meet him at the Kochrab Ashram in Ahmedabad for further discussion. Soon after he joined Gandhi in his Ashram. As later said by Vinoba, he found in Mahatma the peace of the Himalayas united with the revolutionary fervor of Bengal. After joining the Ashram, Vinoba conformed to its rigorous and austere life. He worked in the kitchen, in the workshop and in the garden like any other inmate. One day he was heard loudly reciting verses from the Gita and the Upanishads early in the morning at 4'o clock. In the following days Gandhiji and Vinoba worked together grinding corn, cleaning toilets and studying the philosophy of Gita and Upanishads. There were several historic developments taken place between 1934 to 1940. Even though the Congress was critical of the Government of India Act, 1935, it decided to contest the Elections. It had convincing majority, seven out of eleven provinces. It had done well so far the administration in these provinces was concerned. But as the war aims of the Raj were not made clear to the Congress, its Ministers resigned. Then it launched the Individual Satyagraha under the leadership of Mahatma Gandhi ji. Vinoba was courted arrest on 21st October, 1940 during the First Satyagraha.

Acharya Vinoba Bhave's name was flashed in banner headlines on the front pages of newspapers in India as well as abroad in October, 1940. After the outbreak of the Second World War, the British Government had drawn India into this global holocaust without seeking the consent of the nation. Therefore, the only alternative before the Indian National Congress was to non-cooperate with all efforts to mobilize the support of the Indian people in favor of the War. It was decided in the Congress Working Committee after serious discussions to seek guidance from Mahatma Gandhi regarding the pattern of civil resistance to be launched against the British Government. Gandhiji after considering all the aspects decided to launch an individual satyagraha movement as distinguished from mass civil disobedience as on earlier occasions. In view of the political conditions persistent at that time, Mahatma wanted to lay greater emphasis on quality rather than quantity. On this criterion, Mahatma selected Vinoba as the first Satyagrahi – civil resister – and Jawaharlal Nehru, the second. Before announcing Vinoba's name as the first Satyagrahi, Gandhiji decided to go to Paunar and seek his consent. He told Vinoba :

> "The Congress has asked me to launch a struggle against the British Government and has left the mode and time of the movement to me. I propose to begin with individual satyagraha, and I have your name in mind as the first Satyagrahi."
>
> "As you deem proper", was Vinoba's humble reply. "Do I take it that you agree to my proposal?" "Bapu, I do." "You must be busy with a variety of activities in your Ashram. I hope you will be able to free yourself from them." "I carry no load on my head", put in Vinoba. "I am as prepared to obey your call here and now even as I would be, if the Yamraj – God of Death – had sent for me." Both Jamnalal Bajaj and Mahadev Desai who had accompanied Gandhiji to Pavnar were deeply touched by this rare example of voluntary obedience and dedication.

Introducing Vinoba to the people of India and the World, Gandhiji issued a comprehensive statement on 5th October, 1940:

> "Who is Vinoba Bhave and why he has been selected for offering individual civil disobedience in 1940? He is an undergraduate, having left college after my return to India in 1916. He is a Sanskrit scholar. He joined the Ashram almost at its inception. He was among the first members. In order to better quality himself, he took one year's leave to prosecute further studies in Sanskrit. And practically at the same hour at which he had left the Ashram a year before, he walked into it without notice. I had forgotten that he was due to arrive that day. He has taken part in every menial activity of the Ashram from scavenging to cooking. Thought he has a marvelous memory and is a student by

nature, he has devoted the largest part of his time to spinning in which he has specialized as very few have. He believes in universal spinning being the central activity, which will remove the poverty in the villages and put life into their deadness. Being a born teacher, he has been of the utmost assistance to Ashadevi Aryanayakam of Hindustani Talimi Sangh in her development of the scheme of education through handicrafts. Sri Vinoba has produced a textbook, taking spinning as the handicraft. It is original in conception. He has made scoffers realize that spinning is the handicraft par excellence which lends itself to being effectively used for basic education. He has revolutionized Takli spinning and drawn out its hitherto unknown possibilities. For perfect spinning, probably, he has no rival in all India."

"He has abolished every trace of untouchability from his heart. He believes in communal unity with the same passion that I have. In order to know the best mind of Islam, he gave one year to the study of the Koran in the original. He, therefore, learned Arabic. He found his study necessary for cultivating a living contact with the Muslims living in his neighborhood. He has an army of disciples and workers, who would rise to any sacrifice at his bidding. He is responsible for producing a young man who has dedicated himself to the service of lepers. Though an utter stranger to medicine, this worker has by singular devotion mastered the method of treatment of lepers and is running several clinics for their care. Hundreds owe their cure to his labours. He has published a handbook in Marathi for the treatment of lepers. Vinoba was for years director of the Mahila Ashram in Wardha.

His devotion to the cause of Daridranarayan took him first to a village near Wardha, and now he has gone still further and lives in Pavnar, five miles from Wardha, from where he has established contact with villagers through the disciples he has trained. Vinoba believes in the necessity of the political independence of India. He is an accurate student of history. But he believes that real independence of the villagers is impossible without the constructive programme of which Khadi is the centre. He believes that the spinning wheel is the most suitable outward symbol of non-violence, which has become an integral part in the previous Satyagraha campaigns. He has never been in the limelight on the political platform. With many co-workers he believes that silent constructive work with civil disobedience in the background is far more effective than the already heavily crowded political platform. And he thoroughly believes that non-violent resistance is impossible without a hearty belief in and practice of constructive work."

This is not the first time when Bapu had talked or written about Vinoba. In June 1916, he had informed Vinoba's father at Baroda in course of a brief letter " Your son Vinoba is with me. He has acquired at so tender an age such high-spiritedness and asceticism as took me years of patient labour to do." Gandhiji further wrote in a correspondence to Vinoba, "I dont know what epithet to use in respect of you. Your love and character overwhelm me." In 1917, when Rev. C.F. Andrews was staying at the Sabarmati Ashram, Gandhiji described to him Vinoba's qualities in these words : He is one of the few pearls in the Ashram. They do not come like others to be blessed by the Ashram, but to bless it, not to receive, but to give!". Chakravarthi C. Rajagopalachari in his article in *Young*

India dated 19th July, 1923 described Vinoba as "gentle as an angel, whose soaring spirit has reached the heights of scholarship, philosophy and religion, and yet, whose humility is so genuine and successful that no official who does not know him can discover his greatness."

Vinoba was arrested in 1923 at the time of the Flag Satyagraha started by Jamnalal Bajaj and attracted countrywide attention. Vinoba wrote a letter to Gandhiji giving the details of his work in the villages around Wardha and seeking his valuable guidance. Gandhiji in his reply addressed him as Kritayugi Vinoba and observed : If something must be said, it is enough to say that the fiery ordeal you are going through would build a bridge between heaven and earth!" Sometime later, Gandhiji again wrote to Vinoba in his own hand : "Your love and faith fill my eyes with tears of joy. I may or may not deserve them. But they are sure to do you infinite good. You will be instrument of great service." Even though Vinoba participated in the Civil Disobedience Movement in 1930 at Wardha, the British Government did not arrest him. But in 1932 he was sent to Dhulia jail in Khandesh, Maharashtra, where he delivered Talks on the Gita to the fellow prisoners every Sunday. These talks were later published in book form as *Gita Pravachanen,* which has been translated in all the Indian regional languages and also in English, Sanskrit and Nepali. During the individual satyagraha movement, Vinoba delivered a speech against participation in the Second World War on 17th October, 1940. For this he was arrested and sentenced to three months simple imprisonment. Jawaharlal Nehru who was chosen as the second satyagrahi was arrested even before he offered a formal satyagraha and was convicted for four years rigorous imprisonment. The movement thereafter gathered momentum in different parts of the country. After the completion of the sentence, Vinoba again offered

Satyagraha and was again jailed for six months imprisonment. In the third time, he secured a full one year's jail term. It was during this period that Vinoba found time to write out his thesis entitled *Swaraj Shastra* or *A Grammar of Politics.* When Gandhiji launched the "Quit India" movement in 1942, Vinoba was again put behind bars on the very first day. He was this time kept under detention for three years, first at the Vellore Central Prison in Sounth India and later at the Seoni Jail in Madhya Pradesh. On his release in 1944, Vinoba returned to his Ashram at Pavnar and quietly joined his constructive work in the rural areas including scavenging in Surgaon village, four miles from his Ashram. Daily he used to walk down to Surgaon with a pickaxe on his shoulders to do sanitation work without bothering the heat or cold, sur or rain.

After the assassination of Mahatma Gandhi on 30th January, 1948, an all India Conference was convened in Sevagram early in March that year. This was attended by all the important political leaders including Rajendra Prasad, Jawaharlal Nehru, Abul Kalam Azad, J.B. Kripalani, Shankarrao Deo and top ranking Gandhian constructive workers like Vinoba Bhave, Kakasaheb Kalelkar, R.R. Diwakar, Dada Dharmadhikari, P.C. Ghosh and Jayaprakash Narayan. During this Conference only Vinoba initiated the formation of the Sarvodaya Samaj, a worldwide organisation of all those who believed in the Gandhian principle of the "purity of the means". In the course of deliberations, Nehru looked to Vinoba for guidance and called himself a "camp-follower". On Nehru's request Vinoba soon left for Delhi to work among the refugees and lend a helping hand to the Government of India in the work of relief and rehabilitation. He paid special attention and care to urgent needs of the Meos Muslims in the Gurgaon district of Punjab. Vinoba also travelled by road and train to other parts of the country to spread the message of love, compassion and sympathy.

Vinoba stands as a symbol for the struggle of the good against the evil, of spiritual against the mundane. He was a spiritual visionary, whose spirituality had a pragmatic stance with intense concern for the deprived. He was a brilliant scholar who could knowledge accessible to ordinary people. He was Gandhi's ardent follower, who could retain originality in thinking. As the former President of India Dr. S. Radhakrishnan pointed out "Indeed his life represents harmonious blend of learning, spiritual perception and compassion for the lowly and the lost."

References

- Publications Division, Acharya Vinoba Bhave, 1955 India.
- Shah Kanti, Vinoba: Life and Mission, 1979, Varanasi.
- Shriman Narayan, Vinoba: His Life and Mission, 1970-71, Bombay.
- Shri P.D. Tandon, Vinoba Bhave : The Man and his Mission.

2

Bhoodan Movement

Vinoba delivered five important speeches at the Shivrampalli Sammelan. He desired the constructive workers to take to agriculture and develop faith in physical labour. Additionally, they should try to run their institutions on the basis of self sufficiency and without the use of money. Vinoba further suggested that peace brigades – shanti senas – should be organized in eaeh village for self protection through non-violent resistance. Every effort should be made to infuse the spirit of honesty and integrity in public life. He also indicated in these speeches that for augmenting agricultural production in the country, labourers should be paid wages in kind, in the form of grain and other consumer needs. Vinoba repeated his earlier suggestion that the Government should realize land revenue in kind in place of cash. Furthermore, the Government should undertake to train all adults in hand-spinning, and weaving should be organized by the State agencies free of charge. This would help in popularizing khadi and enabling the people to produce cloth for their annual requirements.

Vinoba, at the Sarvodaya Conference placed a new sutra – formula, covering five items of constructive work – internal purity, village sanitation, reverence for physical labour, peace army and yarn-contribution. He urged the workers to implement this five-point programme in all sincerity. In the concluding session, Vinoba also announced that he intended going to the Telangana region where the Communists on the one hand and the Army on the other hand created a complicated situation. He wanted to study the facts at first hand, before returning to Wardha. Vinobha remarked "What would happen during this sojourn or thereafter was known only to God."

On the Ramnavami day, 15th April, 1951, Vinoba embarked on his pilgrimage of peace. He was accompanied by Damodardas, Mahadevitai, Madalsadevi and one or two other workers of the region. He refused to accept the protection of the Army or the police during this Padyatra which proved to be unique in the annals of the Sarvodaya movement in Independent India. Vinoba could hardly sleep during the night. He was profoundly influenced by the turn of events at Pochampalli. As he was preparing to leave for another village next morning, Ramchandra Reddy went to his cottage, touched his feet and handed over to him a written declaration about his donation. From that day onwards, Vinoba toured on foot from village to village asking for land donations. The word "Bhoodan" was, in truth, used by him at the next halt after Pochampalli. Some days later, Yajna was added to Boodan. In every village, land donations poured in, and Vinoba was convinced that God wanted him to continue this movement tirelessly with faith and resolution. These voluntary gifts of land in many villages of Telangana transformed the whole atmosphere in a miraculous manner. In places where the people were afraid to assemble, owing to the terror of the Army during day and the fear of the Communists during night, thousands attended Vinoba's evening prayers and listed to his discourses in pin-drop silence. Hatred and violence gradually yielded place to love and co-operation among the people. Vinoba asked the villagers to become self-reliant and fearless. Vinoba's party since trekked from village to village in Telangana, the people would innocently say: "Gandhi has been reincarnated". Some others would exclaim: Gandhi's son is coming to meet us." And yet others remarked: "Here comes a God who gives away land". Even before he reached the next village at sunrise on the following day, the landlords were, more or less, prepared to be 'looted with love'. In the starting, the majority of donors were small and middle class peasants, but as Bhoodan rolled on, richer farmers also volunteered their donations and received Vinoba with genuine faith and respect.

Vinoba dedicated himself to the propagation of new kind of social revolution in India. The vehicle he originated for this work, known as the Bhoodan Movement, has as its primary tangible objective "land for the landless." Its intangible implications are even more significant. Emphasizing a voluntary giving – first of land and more recently also of cash, kind, labor, intelligence, life and of whole villages – he has sought to bring his people to a fuller realization of man's nobler nature.

Vinoba explained the concept of Bhoodan to his rural audience in a variety of ways. When people came to receive him with flowers and garlands, he would say: "These flowers are beautiful; but earth, the mother of these flowers, is even more beautiful. While flowers are meant for worship, I ask for land only. I am your son, a member of your family. If you have four sons, I am the fifth and should be given my due share". To others he would appear: "In olden days, our ancestors used to perform Yagnas in order to restore peaceful conditions. To remove bitterness in the villages, I have started the Bhoodan Yagna and everyone should take part in it for the welfare of the masses." To the doubting Thomases he would affirm his unflinching faith in the goodness of man: "I believe that hearts do change, and non-violence alone is the remedy for all our ills. A psychological revolution like this cannot be brought about by violence. It can be ushered in only through the methods of Buddha, Christ and Gandhiji". Vinoba even accepted land donations from the poor. At one place, a man owning only one acre donated a Guntha or one fortieth of an acre. It was not very clear as to how this small piece of land could be utilized. Vinoba said "I would ask the owner to till that small piece of land as a trustee and utilize the production for the benefit of the poor. That a man who owns only one acre is prompted to part with a Guntha out of it is certainly a revolution. Wherever there is an ideological revolution, life marches towards progress Vinoba described Bhoodan Yagna in another village meeting "as an application of non-violence, an experiment in transformation of life itself". He further explained that non violence was not opposed to modern science. "Science can transform this earth into heaven, but it can do so only in combination with non-violence. If science and violence are joined together, the world will be shattered to pieces."

Besides the donations of the lands, Vinoba conveyed to the villagers the imperative need of becoming self-reliant by setting up village and cottage industries: "Without cottage industries, mere possession of land by the peasant will not solve his problem. If the agriculturists take to producing finished goods from the raw material obtaining in the villages, they will be able to save themselves."

Vinoba's Telangana tour lasted 51 days and he passed through some 200 villages and received 12,200 acres of land for distribution among the landless. He formed a committee of three consisting of Kodandaram Reddy, Laxmibai Sangam and Keshava Rao (Convenor). This committee was designated as Shoonya Samiti signifying that the three workers would function in a spirit of humility and service. During this peace pilgrimage, Vinoba was also able to settle about 500 village feuds and addressed over 200,000 of people. Not even a single village where he had camped had refused land gifts, the average being 240 acres a day. Even the Nizam gave away some land to Vinoba.

Vinoba reached Sevagram on 26 June 1951 while returning from Telangana. He had left for his memorable trek to Shivrampalli from Sevagram on 06th March and was back to Gandhiji's Ashram after an eventful journey on foot lasting 112 days. Vinoba could have gone to Paunar directly, but preferred to halt at Sevagram to meet Ashram inmates and workers and students of the basic education colony. Addressing the staff and students, Vinoba said: I had started my Padayatra with your good wishes which stood me in very good stead during the Telangana tour. I am happy to be here again in your midst today." On his way to Paunar next morning, Vinoba halted at Gopuri for a brief period. Addressing the workers he made a meaningful observation: "In the years to come, the main tussle in the world will be between the two ideologies of Sarvodaya and Marxism. It is impossible to strike any compromise between these two ideologies. If we do not carry on our work properly, Communism is bound to make inroads in to our public life. We should, therefore, recognize the signs of the times and introduce radical changes in our institutions." On reaching Paramdham Ashram, Vinoba was happy to meet his colleagues after three months. He informed them that Bhoodan had become a reality only because of the confidence he had been able to gain at Paunar in the pursuit of kanchan-mukti programmes. He added: "I have no intention of continuing the work of receiving land-gifts. I am now regarded as the reincarnation of vaman, and will gladly receive donations."

The Bhoodan Movement started by Vinoba Bhave was a new innovation in the socio-economic life of the teeming millions living in more than six lakhs of villages. Though his speeches, writings and regular contacts with the affluent people holding several acres of land. Vinoba Bhave requested them to part with a sizeable portion of it so that it could be given to the landless. For this mission he moved from village to village, from one end of the country to the other. The response in several regions was quite favourable and people donated their land in the Bhoodan Yajna. People offered their wells, implements and several other articles used in farming. Vinoba Bhave distributed these donations among the needy and advised them to work for better production. As a result of his efforts, several families which were landless, received the ownership of land and in a few years their economic status was enhanced. In some cases, unproductive land in the far-flung areas was donated. It gave out less dividends but on the whole the donation was beneficial for the receiver. Bhave knew the fact that the landless labourer was the victim of the landlord since ages. His economic means were so meager that he could hardly live. His family was always at the mercy of the landlord and the money-lender. Vinoba wanted to remove these age-old shackles of the landless laborer and wished for him a socio-economic status worthy of the society in which he was to live.

Vinoba after his release from the Dhulia jail, proceeded to Wardha. Since the Satyagraha Ashram had been banned and locked by the Government during the 1932 Civil

Disobedience Movement, he stayed with some of his colleagues in a room near the Cotton Market for a couple of months. During his imprisonment, Vinoba was convinced more than ever that real social and economic progress in the country was impossible of achievement without paying special attention to the villages. He therefore, on return, decided to organize intensive work in the villages of Wardha Taluk. He established an organisation for the purpose and named it Gramseva Mandal – Village Service Association – with its headquarters at Nalwadi, a village of 800 population and about a mile and half from Wardha town, mostly inhabited by landless labour, especially the Harijans.

Vinoba Bhave shifted to the Nalwadi village on 25 December, 1932 and wrote the following letter to Mahatma Gandhiji:

> Nalwadi, a village about a mile and half from Wardha, is inhabited only by Harijans. Wardha Ashram will complete the twelfth year of its existence soon a yuga has completed its full circle. Experiences during the period have been satisfactory. Egoism has faded away. The conviction that God alone has grown on us. For so many years I did not live in Wardha, but at your behest. To me nothing counts in this world save your blessings. I may say that it has been my constant endeavor during these twelve years to observe the Ashram vows. Yet I experience many failings within me. God has blessed me much more than my devotion towards Him deserves.
>
> I know your blessings are even there to protect me. Even so, I write this letter to beseech them. Please do take care of this humble servant of yours. Kindly secure for him from Providence the fitness to be worthy of a sacrifice in your great cause. If

there are any directions for the future, please do let me know.

Vinoba's respectful Pranams

Gandhiji was deeply touched by this letter to which he replied as under:

Chi. Vinoba,

Your love and faith full made my eyes with tears of joy. I may or may not diverse them. But they are sure to do you infinite good. You will be an instrument of great service. It is good that you have shifted to Nalwadi.

My suggestions for the future are as follows: Without insisting on avoidance of milk, take care of your body. Your present duty is to spread an atmosphere against untouchability. Find time to read whatever I write on different occasions. It does not amount to very much. Keep on writing letters to me; even a letter a week will do.

Bapu's blessings

Vinoba initially lived in Nalwadi in a very simple hut with walls made of ordinary bamboos. It had no bath-room attached to it and there were hardly any other facilities. Even the floor was kuccha and was occasionally plastered with cow dung. Some time later, another ordinary bamboo structure with tiled roof was put up as a kitchen. At Nalwadi, Vinoba made special experiments on hand-spinning with takli or a spindle which would cost the rural population only a few annas and on which by working for eight hours, a person could earn about 2 annas a day. Vinoba used to write occasionally to Gandhiji about his experiences on the takli. One would scarce believe that the spread on the takli was faster than on the charka. In the beginning, even Gandhiji did not accept this claim. But Vinoba's arithmetic ultimately proved to be incontrovertible. According to Vinoba's scheme off rural reconstruction, each worker toured about a dozen villages intensively every fortnight. He had with him a detailed list of these villages, indicating their population, social condition and their economic problems. People were trained in hand-spinning and weaving so that they could not only earn some daily wages for their own maintenance but also manufacture khadi for local consumption. Some of the main workers of the Gramseva Mandal were Manohar Divan (whom Gandhiji had described in his statement on Vinoba in 1940 as 'a young man who has dedicated himself to the service of lepers') Gopalrao Kale, Babaji Moghe, gopalrao Valunjkar, Vallabhswami, Tukaram Bua, Chhotelal Ramdasbhai, Dilip Kumar and Shankarrao Chowdhury.

The Nalwadi Ashram consisted of about seven or eight workers, including some women. They held morning and evening prayers, did community spinning, cooked food, washed clothes and utensils, did sanitation and scavenging work and also spent a few hours on the study of the Ramayana, the Gita, Jnaneshwari and the Upanishads. Vinobaji taught Gitai to men and women who joined his classes. The evening prayers were attended by quite a few persons living in Nalwadi village. As a result of untiring efforts of Vinoba and his band of workers, 43 temples and 300 village wells were thrown open to Mandal for the removal of untouchability made a good impact on the village communities. Gramseva Mandal's intention was to saturate all the villages within Wardha taluka with khadi so that the weaker sections could not only obtain some supplementary income during the off seasons but also become self-sufficient at least in their cloth requirements. The number of villages in Wardha Tehsil was about 310, and the total population about 2 lakhs.

Ashram Vritta, a monthly bulletin was published under Vinoba's direction from time to time. It contained useful information in Marathi about the work of the Ashram and the four of the workers in the Wardha villages. Apart from this, Vinoba used to write letters to Bapu and Jamnalal Bajaj about his experiments. Once Vinoba had objected to hand-spinning of fine yearn. He had compared coarse yarn with Valmiki's Ramayana and fine yarn to Banabhatt's Kadambari. Gandhiji however, disagreed with this view and addressed an interesting letter to Vinoba on 24 October, 1932:

> "The comparison with Banabhatta and Valmiki is not right. Our forefathers forced the poor to produce Dacca muslin to gratify the delicate tastes of people who loved luxury. Let us atone for their sin by spinning as yajna yarn of the finest count and offer it to the Lord. The art in both cases is the same, but in olden times it ministered to selfishness. Let our art help in spreading the spirit of service. It is necessary to revive the old skill in order to popularize khadi among all classes of people. We should prove that what was possible then in the days of slavery can be done in the age of freedom too."
>
> If this reasoning appeals to you, I need not explain to you why I put down 20 counts as the minimum for a voluntary spinner to achieve. There is, however, nothing inviolate about this figure; it is not laid down as a fixed principle. It is only a test of the devotion of the voluntary spinner.
>
> If I have not been able to explain my point of view, you may write to me again and ask me. I have no doubt in the matter, but I cannot rest at ease till I have satisfied you.

About Vinoba's work in the villages, Gandhiji wrote in the same letter:

> "I realize very well how exceedingly difficult it is to go into the villages. However, despite the difficulties, we must go. I, therefore, very much like the beginning you are making."

In the course of letter addressed to Jamnalalji in August, 1934 Vinoba observed:

> "I experience unusual inspiration while spinning on takli so much so that my mother, gita and takli have literally become synonymous terms in my mental dictionary. *Ai*-mother-contains all the rich experience I gathered at home during childhood. Gita incorporates all the wisdom from the Vedas and the tradition of saints in India. And takli reveals to me all the experience gained by Bapu's guidance."

In another letter, written in February, 1935, Vinoba stated:

> "You have asked me about my daily programme. The fact of the matter is that I draw inspiration only from two items – repeating God's name and spinning the whole day. All the rest, including study, writing, discussions and speeches, appear to me to be insignificant as a zero. In essence, God's remembrance and spinning are almost identical to me. If zeros are added to one, they go on adding strength; but without the one, all remain merely zeros. I, therefore, take care of the one, i.e. daily prayers and spinning."

Writing to Radhakrishna Bajaj in October, 1936, Vinoba remarked:

"My mind is full of takli these days. At present I feel almost like a child. I, therefore, like small things. Just as a child likes small utensils, small bread and small sweets. I also feel attracted towards small items. I have with me a small Gita and a small takli. I also require a small *dhunki* – carding apparatus."

At the instance of Jamnalalji, Vinoba also spent some time in revising Gitai, the Marathi translation of the Gita. Accordingly, three or four editions of the Gitai were published by the Gramseva Mandal and Vinoba made several alteration in each edition. Jamnalalji also requested Vinoba to edit the manuscript of his discourses on the Gita given in Dhulia jail. Gita in pravachanen was first printed in the original Marathi and subsequently translated into Hindi and other Indian languages.

In another letter, Vinoba expressed his definite view that "constructive work will not make any headway until some intellectuals engaged themselves in physical labour out of their own free will". In regard to weaving, he mentioned the following points:

(i) We should prepare the best possible slivers and make them freely available to those villagers who desire to learn spinning;

(ii) At least half a dozen workers should be engaged in spinning at one place, so that similar community-spinning could be organized in the rural areas. Continuous experiments should be conducted in spinning, carding and weaving in all our centers.

(iii) Now workers should be trained every year for expanding our work;

(iv) The quality of khadi produced by us should be of the highest order;

(v) There should be an atmosphere of constant research and study around me in the Ashram. In the absence of such an atmosphere, I cannot carry on my daily activities.

In the year 1932, after Satyagraha, the Government kept Vinoba's Ashram sealed for about a year. Even when the buildings were released by the authorities, Vinoba did not like to re-start the Ashram in its old form. After careful consideration, it was transformed into Gramseva Mandal for doing intensive village work, and its buildings were made available to Mahila Ashram, a women's institution of an all-India nature where the wives, sisters and daughters of political and constructive workers received education under the direction of Gandhiji and Vinoba. Earlier, a *Kanya Shala* – Girls' school – had been started on an ad hoc basis in the staff quarters of the adjoining High School. This was mainly for the daughters of various workers engaged in educational and constructive work. After closure, girl-students of the Sabarmati Ashram were also sent to this *Kanya Shala*, later called Ashram at Wardha. Important national leaders visited the institution from time to time. It was from here that Gandhiji commenced his historic Harijan tour on 07th November, 1933. This was subsequently merged into the Mahila Ashram. Even while living in Nalwadi for conducting the Gramseva Mandal activities, Vinoba used to take classes in the Mahila Ashram and join the evening prayers. It was mainly due to Vinoba's active interest in this institution that it soon grew into a first-rate educational campus for girls as well as adult women. It was a purely residential institution and students from almost all the States of India were attracted towards it. A large number of girls from Nepal also joined it due to the efforts of Tulsi Mehr, a Nepalese constructive worker who had lived in the Sabarmati Ashram in the early twenties. Mahila Ashram has been responsible for training up a good number of women workers on Gandhian lines, and they are still working in different States with excellent achievements to their credit. Vinoba and his colleagues were also placed in change of a boys' high school which was run by Jamnalalji and Jajuji. It was formerly known as Marwadi Vidyalaya where Gandhiji, after the Nagpur Congress Session of 1920, first asked the staff and students to sever all connections with Government in regard to recognition and degrees. In 1926 this Vidyalaya was converted into a 'Rastriya Vidya Mandir', with independent courses of study on national lines. Many students and teachers naturally left it, and only about 25 students, including Kamalnayan Bajaj, Dattoba Dastane, Kunder Diwan, Bhanu Panse, Budhsen and Kishan Jaju, continued to pursue their studies here. The curriculum included the study of Marathi, Sanskrit, Hindi and English besides a general knowledge of economics, politics and sociology. Special emphasis was laid on the study of the Gita, Ramayana, and the Upanishads. The Marathi Bhajans of Tukaram, Jnanadev formed in important part of the syllabus. The Vidyalaya had to be closed down during the Satyagraha of 1930. It reopened for some time after the Gandhi-Irwin Pact, but also finally wined up in 1932.

The main criticism against the Wardha Satyagraha Ashram had been that it was cut-off from the mainstream of public life and tended to become some sort of an island, isolated from the people. The Gramseva Mandal, therefore, was organized on a entirely different basis, and its chief aim was to forge living links with the rural population on the foundation of self-reliance and co-operation. These basic objectives of the Mandal have been attained over the years with notable success. The worship at Gopuri, manufacturing traditional and Ambar Charkhas along with the accessories, is one of the biggest in the country today and is run in an efficient manner. Its management is in the hands of an executive committee which adopts various resolutions on the basis of unanimity and not by majority vote. For many years it experimented with yarn currency for its transactions in place of metallic or paper currency. The workers obtained a variety of consumer goods from the Swarajya Bhandar co-operative stores – by paying for them in hanks of self-spun yarn. This was, indeed, a novel experiment which worked for several years with fairly satisfactory results. This was inaugurated by Mahatma Gandhiji himself in March 1942.

As an integral part of the Gramseva Mandal's programme Vinoba used to organize every year a khadi-yatra in one of the work-centres of Wardha Taluka. This was in nature of an annual conference of constructive workers engaged in khadi and other allied activities. Meetings held at the Khadi-yatra were largely attended by the villages of the neighbouring areas. The session lasted two days, and besides speeches, there were competitions for spinning and weaving and prizes were awarded to the winners in the form of spinning wheels and other equipment. An exhibition of khadi and village industries was also organized on this occasion. At these meetings the workers related their experiences of constructive work in different villages and discussed various problems in order to find practical solutions. These khadi-yatras continued till 1941 and served a definite purpose. They were helpful in generating an atmosphere of self-sufficiency and dignity of labour amongst the rural population. The workers looked forward to these annual meetings because they provided an opportunity of enriching their own programme in the countryside. From letters written by Vinoba Bhave to important constructive workers, it is evident that he supervised various activities which an eye on efficiency and correct idealism. In one of the letters he complains about the lack of sanitation in the dairy at Nalwadi. In another communication, he expresses his disapproval of the introduction of piece-work in the workshop and rules out a proposal to allow the workers to complete their assignments at home. Such a system, he fears, may tempt the workers to get a portion of their work done through others in the form of a sub-contract, resulting in economic exploitation. To enable to spin on the takli for eight hours without any intervals of rest, Vinoba practiced spinning alternately with both the hands. When the right hand was tired, he would spin with the left and vice versa. Sometime later at Paunar, he introduced Tunai – hand carding. This reduced the need for a carding machine and provided gainful work to the unemployed. The slivers prepared out of this hand carded cotton were found to be quite satisfactory. With regard to the teaching of languages in the Satyagrah Ashram or later at Nalwadi, Vinoba's main emphasis was on learning one language thoroughly – its grammar, diction, pronunciation and usage. He has been of the definite opinion that if a student learns one language in a thorough manner, it will be possible for him to pick up other languages quite easily. Vinoba would commence the teaching of Sanskrit with the Gita; English he would start with the Bible, and Marathi with Jnaneshwari and the Bhajans of Tukaram.

Gandhiji looked upon Vinoba both as his son as well as a Guru. He was all praise for him and expressed his inner sentiments to his colleagues from time to time. Bapu addressed him as Kritayugi Vinoba in a letter written on 19th September, 1932 from the Yervada Jail. Kritayuga literally means 'the golden age', and Gandhiji used the epithet for Vinoba because he was engaged in selfless activities in the service of the Divine. Gandhiji's letter with wit and humour of a rare kind, and is reproduced below:

Yervada Jail
September 19,1932

Kritayugi Vinoba,

We need not envy you for living in the Kritayuga, for we too, have with us the Kritayugi Sardar and, therefore, rise at least a few inches higher than you. Do you know that the Sardar keeps walking most of the time ? He would, if he could, even eat walking and spin walking. Even though an old man, he tries to learn the Gita by heart while walking. For improving his pronunciation he should be sent to you, and you given a cane to correct him. But you are not likely to have that good fortune in the immediate future.

You seem to have mastered the art of holding out false assurances to the poor! When a poor man like me had been pining for a letter from you, you did not write at all; and now when I am getting ready to lie down on my deathbed, you write to say, now that I have started writing, I shall write regularly. But may be I am destined to survive this ordeal, since the vows of Kritayugis are not known to remain unfulfilled. If I do leave this bed, I will expect to hear regularly from you.

Through this bit of jestings, I have diverted my mind for a while from the letters I have been wiritng on serious matters and, also suggested that your activities call for no criticism. Keep me informed about them.

If I come out unscathed in body and soul through this ordeal and if there is something to write about,

I shall write to you, will preserve your letter.

-Bapu's blessings

While undertaking the historic march to Dandi in March 1930 in connection with Salt Satyagraha, Gandhiji had announced his decision not to return to the Sabarmati Ashram till Swaraj was achieved. The Ashram was, accordingly, converted into a Harijan educational institution. Even when Gandhiji came to Ahmedabad after the end of the movement, he stayed for a while at Gujarat Vidyapith, and not at Sabarmati. Jamnalal Bajaj took this opportunity of inviting the Mahatma to make Wardha his permanent headquarters. In consequence, Gandhiji used to go to Wardha quite often and stayed in the Prayer-hall at Mahila Ashram and later at Maganwadi, the headquarters of the All India Village Industries Association. It was on 30 April, 1936 that Gandhiji walked down to Sevagram village, four miles from Wardha, to settle down there. Early in 1938, Vinoba's health deteriorated considerably, causing anxiety to Jamnalalji and Gandhiji. Vinoba was advised by Bapuji to go to a hill-station for rest and convalescence. Vinoba agreed to consider the matter. He one day went to Pavnar, a village on the Nagpur road, about six miles from Wardha. Jamnalal Bajaj had constructed a villa on the bank of river Dham for occasional rest. Vinoba liked this place and informed Gandhiji that he had selected a 'hill station' for himself. At Paunar, Vinoba used his own 'pathy' to regain normal health. He worked hard for several hours a day in the adjoining fields which were full of relics of the capital city of Pavan kingdom which existed in this area more than 1500 years ago. He would prepare butter out of groundnuts and eat plenty of vegetables grown in the Ashram. Vinoba increased the intake of milk as well. As a result, his weight steadily increased from 90 lbs to 120 lbs. Within six months.

At Paunar that Vinoba sought the assistance of a Muslim scholar to learn Arabic in order to study the Holy Quran in the original. Subsequently, Vinoba prepared a book of selections from the Quran and published it under the title 'The essence of the Quran'. Hindi, Urdu and English editions of this collection were brought out by the Sarva Seva Sangh. They were very useful in acquainting constructive workers with the basic principles of Quran and removing a number of misconceptions about the Islamic religion.

Vinoba also commenced at Paunar a new experiment of 'God-realization' through a Brahma Vidya Mandir, consisting exclusively of unmarried girl-students drawn from different parts of the country. Vinoba has often remarked that this institution will, perhaps, be his last activity. The inmates of the Mandir lead a life of self-sufficiency by producing all their requirements locally with their own labour without the assistance of any servants. They also spend several hours a day on self-study of religious books, including the Gita and the Upanishads. Vinoba believes that the knowledge of the Supreme through bread-labour and self-reliance could be attained more easily by women rather than man. "In the troubled but dynamic scene that is India today" observed Pandit Nehru in a message to the Sarvodaya Conference, "the frain figure of Vinobaji stands like a rock of strength, modest and gentle, yet with something of the vision of the future in his eyes". "It is not for us, smaller folk, to judge him whether we agreed with him or disagreed in some matter, for he is above these minor judgements. He represents, as none else does, the spirit and tradition of Gandhiji and of India."

On the occasion of Vinoba's 68th birthday celebrations in New Delhi, Nehru said "It is the good luck of the present generation that we have a person of Vinobaji stature in our midst. In fact, no one in the wide world today could be likened to him. His way of life brings to one's mind the values which Gandhiji stood for Acharya Vinoba is uniquely Indian, and yet he possesses a keen insight into contemporary trends. He is like a beacon showing us the right path and correcting us whenever we go wrong."

The unique personality of Vinoba is a rare synthesis of profound knowledge, deep devotion and sustained action. While his scholarship in the Vedas, the Upanishads and other Sanskrit scriptures is almost matchless, and his knowledge of more than sixteen Indian and European languages is phenomenal, Vinoba possesses a loving, compassionate and devout heart which invariably makes a noticeable impact on the people. Besides, he has traveled on foot for more than thirteen years in different parts of India, covering a total distance of 36,500 miles – more than the circumference of the earth. During this Padayatra, he collected 4.4 million acres of land as free gifts from the poor, middle-class and richer peasants.

The day India attained her political freedom marked the beginning of a new era and offered her responsibilities of quite a different order. It was a difficult task for the country to organize its social and economic life in the context of the developing and ever-changing world. India was not well prepared to take on the new task. Two centuries of British rule had practically shattered the economy of the country in more than one ways. The village autonomy was broken and replaced by a new system of political organization in which village units were the least recognized. The cottage industries were annihilated and the self-reliant economy was reduced to an economy of dependence and subjection. The Britishers left the country in turmoil. The situation was aggravated by the ill-conceived demand of the Muslims for an independent State which culminated in the division of this sub-continent into two parts: India and Pakistan. There was no geographical justification for the creation of the binary country, Pakistan, consisting of two isolated wings, the East Bengal and the west Punjab, separated by one thousand miles of India territory. It was a purely political decision based on the religion-founded two-nation concept. But this theory could not stand the test of the time and the geographical absurdity of East Pakistan came to an end with the emergence of a democratic, secular and sovereign State of Bangla Desh. The truncated India of 1947-48 had a shattered economy. The division led to an unreasonable distribution of land and population. "As a result of the partition India had nearly 81 percent of the total population of undivided India and nearly 77 percent of the total area." The net population influx was greater in India by 2.5 million persons in comparison to that in Pakistan. The country lost some of the finest wheat, rice and jute producing areas and added relatively a larger urban population. Hardly had the ink dried on the partition deed, then the country faced a great influx of population – unprecedented in the history of the world. Nobody could have imagined that "more than sixteen million persons, i.e. more than twice the population of Australia or more than the entire population of Canada would be involved in the post-partition Indo-Pakistan migration." This migration resulted in bloodshed and hatred and adversely affected the development of the nascent economy.

The colossal refugee problem was unparalleled in the human history. Never before had such mass transfer of population taken place. India faced the "Great Displacement" of population in a short period of less than six months. It is said that 1.4 million Grecian people from Asia Minor and Turkey were once transferred after World War I, but that was achieved over a period of eighteen months. In this respect the great Indo-Pak migration of 1947-48 had the unique characteristics of suddenness, rapidly and vastness. It affected India more than Pakistan as the pressure of population of displaced persons was greater in India. The economy, as a consequence, was thrown out of gear. The gloomy picture of independence was further darkened by the passing away of the father of the nation. The day of 30th January, 1948 marked the end of the earthly pilgrimage of Mahatma Gandhi. The apostle of peace and non-violence had to sacrifice himself to the bullet shot so that the unhappy chapter of Hindu-Muslim tension might come to an end. But even after the great martyrdom this could not be achieved. The sudden departure of Gandhiji was a telling blow to the nation. The newly independent State was in turmoil. There was no leader of such a magnitude who might guide the country's destiny in the hours of peril and darkness. Though Gandhiji had created confidence and initiative in may persons, there was in fact nobody who could measure in heights such a great spiritual leader like him. It was a test for those who believed in the philosophy of Gandhi and his non-violent way of life.

The nation had to decide its future course of action. The first two years of independence were full of great trails and tribulations. The country was entrenched in heavy gloom due to the partition, the mass displacement of the population and the passing away of the Mahatma who stood for the people as the symbol of unity and led the country with his paramount leadership and sacrifice. The problems which confronted people those days left little time for them to think about national development and planning. However, some sporadic attempts were made by the people on the basis of an old Planning Committee and certain plans were put forth to change the structural pattern of the society. The Bombay Plan presented by a few industrialists, the People's Plan given by M.N. Roy, and the Gandhian Plan prepared by Shri Shriman Narain had provided for a line of action in the direction of a planned economy even before the independence. Time made it incumbent upon us thus to choose a system on the basis of which the Five Year Plans might be formulated. The economy of the India was at the cross-roads. Straight in front of her was the far-away goal of hope and aspiration that required sustained labour and efforts for a systematic and comprehensive economic development. Several alternatives offered themselves. One was the "leftist" path of "socialized" economic development with overwhelming State authority as its prime characteristic. The other was the "rightist" road of "highly independent" economic advancement with unrestricted individualism and liberty as its dominant features. India chose the middle path of democratic planning and cooperative endeavor which was supposed to suit her social set-up and was in conformity with her age-old traditions.

Village India, representing the spirit and traditions of ancient Indian life and culture, was plagued with poverty, hunger and landlessness. On the eve of Independence, the Indian peasantry presented a depressing spectacle. Out of every 1000 agriculturists in 1951, 507 were agricultural land-holders of all types and 402 landless agriculturists. The total number of agricultural labour households was 1.79 crores in 1950-51. The first and second Agricultural Labour Enquiry Reports had thrown considerable light on this matter. The average size of the agricultural labour households in 1950-51 was 4.30 persons and rose to 4.40 in 1956-57. The ratio of attached and casual labour households was 10:90 in 1950-51 which increased to 27:73 in 1956-57. The casual adult male workers remained unemployed for ninety days in 1950-51 and 128 days in 1956-57. The average daily wage of casual labour in 1950-

51 was only 109 paise and went down to ninety-six paise in 1956-57. The foremost problem of the country at this juncture was to fight against the forces of stagnation and recession in socio-economic relationships which meant an overall transformation of human values and institutional changes. The problem of land management and organization was to be tackled effectively as the first step in this direction.

The age-old system of landlordism had to come to an end in this period of transition. The landlords so far had worked as the bulwark of the British rule in India. A system based on grants of villages and lease of lands to some influential and "loyal" persons for the payment of land revenue to the Government was adopted first by the Mughals in a feudal form and then by the Britishers who not only created landlords but supported hundreds of dependent Indian rulers in their semi-feudal States. The Britishers could not mix with the masses and so their object was to create a new class of intermediaries for their own benefit. The feudal system had adversely affected the whole economy of the country. The Britishers were interested only in retaining power and to some extent maintaining law and order through the rule of State without any developmental planning. They, therefore, patronized the landlords and created a class of exploiters. The village economy sank deep into the waters of stagnation. The unprecedented famine of 1943 of Bengal explains the discriminating policy in rushing supplies and negligence of villages under the British rule. The rural indebtedness was devastating and it remained a cradle-to-grave companion of the villages. All this, therefore, called for some structural changes in the land management and organization. The abolition of Zamindari was a step towards this direction. When the Congress came to power, it announced its agrarian policy of completely wiping out the feudal system of land management. The method adopted was peaceful and slow. The Zamindari Abolition Acts were passed by different States with a provision for compensation to the affected landlords. The government's decision of getting rid of intermediaries was intended to revitalize the rural organization and cultivation pattern. But unless the whole village structure was changed nothing concrete could have been achieved in the field of economic development.

Through the feudal system was abolished by the State Governments, a new class emerged in the form of "Rentiers". It has come into existence because the abolition of the intermediaries does not mean abolition of the rent receiving class. It is a class which contributes nothing to the production and yet derives income from the landed property. Though legally they are not intermediaries, they receive all the advantage due to the "middleman". The land is cultivated by hired labour and share-cropping is quite common. A system of "produce rent" or "labour rent" is prevalent even after the abolition of Zamindari. The private possession of land is recognized and the old intermediaries have been converted into the so-called "self-cultivating" agriculturists of "Sir" and "Khudkast". In Uttar Pradesh alone, this "private possession of the landlords constituted abut six million out of thirty-three million acres of agricultural land. Thus nearly 15 percent of the entire land was at the very outset declared as the private property of the old landlords." A democratic Government that sanctions the right of ownership can never bring about legislation to the effect of completely abolishing private property. Though pledged for establishing democratic socialism, the Government of India is unable to bring about that social order which demands a total transformation of property rights. A Government by legislation cannot do that. It is possible only through some organized mass movement and well trained public opinion. One cannot deny that feudalism is some form or other is still prevalent in our country. "Though its relative importance varies from State to State it is still a force which matters a lot. In all States, three fourths of the rural population belongs to what is called the weakest section and is still living in an atmosphere of fear and pressure in which caste and feudal traditions combine to undermine their will to assert themselves..."

While narrating his first meeting with Gandhiji at Kochrab Ashram, Vinoba writes: "When I was at Kashi, my main ambition was to go to the Himalayas. Also there was an inner longing to visit Bengal. But neither of the two dreams could be realized. Providence took me to Gandhiji and I found in him not only the peace of the Himalayas but also the burning fervour of revolution typical of Bengal. I said to myself that both of my desires had been fulfilled." Vinoba worked in the kitchen and garden like any ordinary inmate. One day when he was reciting loudly verses from the Gita and the Upanishads in the early morning, then the Ashramites came to know that Vinoba was a profound scholar of sanskirt and religious scriptures. It was Mama Phadke, an inmate from Maharashtra who name Vinayak as Vinoba.

Gandhiji and Vinoba worked together in the Ashram grinding the corn, cleaning latrines and studying the philosophy of the Gita and the Upanishads. Gandhiji once described Vinba to C.F. Andrews as "one of the few pearls in the Ashram, who come there not to be blessed, but to bless it". But Vinoba was all humility and tried to reduce himself to a zero. He has done nothing which would give the slightest impression of 'showing off'. While talking to an inmate, Vinoba said "Only I can know what I have got in the Ashram. It was an early ambition of mine to distinguish myself by some violent deed in the service of the country. But Bapu cured me of that ambition. It is he who has extinguished the volcano of anger and other passions in me. I have been progressing every day of my life in the Ashram." Vinoba's younger brother Balkoba also joined the Ashram after some months. Vinoba was first reluctant to have Balkoba also with him. But later he relented and Balkoba started taking active part in the daily life of the community. In the initial stages, weaving was done with mill yarn in the Ashram. After some years only, the first spinning wheel was brought to the Ashram to practice spinning by hand. Khadi produced during this period was obviously of a very coarse type. After Vinoba's arrival in the Ashram, the art of spinning and weaving underwent a radical change. The mathematical approach of Vinoba has stood him in good stead throughout his life. In the Ashram also he reduced spinning and weaving to an exact science. It was Krishnadas Gandhi, Vinoba's one of the pupils, first taught him how to spin on the Charkha. But very soon he became an expert in the production of Khadi by spending hours together in spinning and weaving. He also taught these crafts to other inmates as well as to the students of the school attached to the Ashram.

Kochrab Ashram was shifted to the Sabarmati. Here also Vinoba continued his work of spinning, weaving as well as teaching. He also worked in kitchen for some months when necessitated. He brought to bear on all types of with efficiency and full devotion. For many months, he also brought water from the Sabarmati river in buckets for use in the Ashram including watering plants. Other inmates noticed this hard work of Vinoba for several weeks and amazed his physical energy despite indifferent health. One day, Gandhiji asked him "How do you stand all this physical labour, Vinoba?". Vinoba replied "It is not so much my body as my will that enables me to undertake this hard work.".

Once the Gujarati teacher of the Ashram was away and Gandhiji desired that Vinoba should teach Gujarati to the students of the National School. However Vinoba hesitated for a while and suggested for another teacher be appointed soon. But Gandhiji wrote back to Vinoba from Navagam on 24th July, 1918: "I have your thought provoking letter. The idea is of course what you have stated. It is also true that to achieve it there should be a Gujarati teacher. But in the absence of such a teacher, it would not be wrong to avail ourselves of a teacher from Maharashtra. Also I would prefer a Marathi teacher who has character to a Gujarati who has none....For the present, therefore, you will have to continue teaching it while keeping the ideal in view." A little later, Mahadev Desai records Gandhiji as saying: "Vinoba is a great man. I have always felt that I am fortunate in my dealings with Maharastrians and Madrasis. Of the latter, there is none now. But no Maharashtrian has ever disappointed me, and among them all Vinoba is beyond praise." Vinoba while taking bath in the river, unfortunately lost balance and fell in to the fast-moving current. He did not raise any scare of some time, but when he found that he was being swept away, he shouted: Convey my namaskars to Bapu and tell him that though Vinoba's body has disappeared, his soul is immortal." Since luck would have it, Vinoba was soon thrown up on a shallow land in midstream and after some respite, swam back to the Ashram.

For some time, Vinoba also functioned as the Superintendent of the hostel attached with National School. It was felt that he due to his stern nature, may deal with the young boys harshly. But everybody was surprised when Vinoba was elected by the students as the superintendent in preference to Kakasaheb Kalelkar. As per school rules, the superintendent is elected every year by students themselves. He used to wake up the hostel boys early in the morning for prayers with great love and affection. He used to recite some shlokas and sing a few songs in a melodious tone, so that the sleeping ones would wake up in an fantastic atmosphere of joy and devotion. His this technique worked very well and Vinoba was soon recognized as a very popular superintendent and also a respected teacher. Vinoba also loved his pupils with all his heart.

Initially Vinoba lived in the verandah of the weaving shed. He used to get up very early in the morning and recite Sanskrit Shlokas from scriptures in a loud but with sweet voice. Later he shifted to a small cottage near Hridayakunj where Gandhiji and Kasturba resided. This Vinobakuti continues to be maintained in the Ashram as a sweet memory of those days After Vinoba left for Wardha, Miraben was occupying it. In the hostel Vinoba also worked as the physical instructor and taught the boys Surya-namaskar and other physical exercises in the morning. He played the games of Kabaddi and Khokho in the Indian style. Games like Cricket were never engaged in the Ashram. The students were basically trained as patriotic citizens for participating in the freedom struggle. IN the Rashtriya Shala attached to the Sabarmati Ashram, all students had to undergo rigorous physical labour at least for three hours a day. Academic subjects were also taught side by side, and every attempt was made to correlate these subjects with manual work and productive crafts.

During his Ashram life, Vinoba did not rest for a single minute during the day. Apart from looking after the boys in the hostel and teaching various subjects to the students of the National School, he also spent a few hours in spinning, weaving, cooking, grinding and preparing the fields with pick-axe for cultivation. Vinoba was a very capable and genius teacher. Prabhudas Gandhi recalls how Kakasaheb and Narhari Parikh were completely fed up with him while teaching grammar. It was ultimately decided to send him to Vinoba who began teaching Sanskrit to Prabhudas not through grammar, but by acquainting with Raghuvansha. Vinoba always insisted on self-study or Swadhyaya for a few hours every day. He always insisted his pupils to imbibe the habit of studying various books by themselves without the assistance of teachers. It was this sprit of self-help and self-reliance in learning academic subjects which was promoted by Vinoba all the time, besides imbuing students with dignity of labour and self-sufficiency in the requirements of food and clothing. He was in favour a single subject taught in a thorough manner against the teaching of too many subjects in a school. He believed this could mould the personality of the boys in the right direction. He used to say that teaching the subjects is not important but educating the boys. Vinoba could recite thousands of poems and verses from Marathi literature without any reference books. Vinoba once decided to carry on spinning for full eight hours a day in order to earn enough for his meals.

Vinoba underwent several changes with his personal dress. During his college days, he used to wear dhoti, shirt, coat and a cap of mill-made swadeshi cloth. When he left his home and proceeded to Varanasi for Sanskrit studies, he gave up the use of coat, but continued his dhoti shirt and cap. Before joining the Gandhi Ashram at Ahmedabad, he had abandoned the cap as well. When hand-spinning and hand-weaving processes at the Ashram culminated in the producing of pure khadi, Vinoba used a dhoti of 35" width and kept the shirt on his shoulders without actually wearing it. Gradually, the shirt was given up and Vinoba stretched a portion of the dhoti on to his shoulders. After some time, he reduced the width of dhoti to 27" and used an untailored upper cloth for covering his body. Since then, his dress has remained almost unchanged. Balkoba narrates an episode which throws a flood of light on Vinoba's personality. While living in the Sabarmati Ashram, Balkoba used to teach music, specially Sitar to some of the students of the National School. He also worked for several hours in the weaving department of which Chhotelal Jain was the Superintendent. One day, there was a clash between Chhotelal and Balkoba over a comparatively minor matter of a technical nature. When Balkoba refused to carry out the directions of Chhotelal, the latter threatened him with disciplinary action. Balkoba felt greatly perturbed and approached Vinoba for his guidance. Vinoba slowly but firmly said: "Chhotelalji is the superintendent of the weaving department. It is essential for everybody working under him to carry out his directions. If each acts in his own light, it will be impossible to run any institution. Your own view may still be correct. But you have done your duty in conveying it to Chhotelalji. The final decision must be his, and you must carry it out." That was the end of the matter and Balkoba acted in the light of this advice.

References

- S. Ram, Vinoba and his Mission.
- Sen Bandhudas, Bhoodan Movement, 1952, Wardha.
- Vinoba Bhave, Principles and Philosophy of the Bhoodan Yagna, 1976.
- Vinoba Bhave, From Bhoodan to Gramdan, 1957, Tanjore.
- Sharma Jagdish Saran, Vinoba and Bhoodan, New Delhi.
- Misra B.R., V for Vinoba : The Economics of Bhoodan Movement.

3

Bhoodan in Broad Spectrum

The revolutionary advance from Bhoodan to Gramdan introduced an important change in Vinobaji's mission. The mission has enabled Vinoba to envisage the spread of his land revolution to the four corners of India. As he made it the mission of his life, he once declared that "My trek is Gramdan. I took a vow last year that I would continue this trek to the end of my life to achieve Gram Swaraj." In his opinion, Gramdan opens the door to a new era of social evolution wherein human beings will perceive and realize the higher values and richer relationships of community sharing. It seeks to establish social order of equality and liberty, of love and sympathy.

Vinoba offers a unique philosophy of villagism. Villagers not to think in terms of land owners and landless peasants. They should think in terms of community, every member of which has valuable contribution to make towards its progress and welfare. The landlord presents a wider field of freedom by offering the entire land in Gramdan to the landless and in doing so widens his own as he rescues himself from bondage of isolation. In one sense, no one owns the land of such a village but in another sense every man owns the entire village, grasps it in his imagination, sees himself as a responsible part of it and the village as a veritable part of his own personality. All the members of a Gramdan village tries to objectify their personality in everything they do and realize that their contribution to the village are themselves, their labour, knowledge and the skill of whatever degree they possess. Vinoba holds that all the persons are sons of the soil. They are nourished by the same land. He further traces back the history of ancient village organizations and offers the same pattern to the new Gramdan villages. *Atharv Veda* has pronounced the same view while praising the motherland. It signifies that all persons are sons of the same soil which provides everything equally as one family. Everybody had to work and people were grouped according to their professions. Gradually, the whole set up undergone a change and people asserted their right of ownership. Now the ownership concept reigns supreme. People have preserved their right to own, sell or mortgage land. In the meantime, the caste and class distinctions have cropped up. Land has become a marketable commodity. All such things have hampered the progress of the country. Vinoba, therefore, calls for discarding the ownership concept. Therefore in Gramdan the right to own land is voluntarily surrendered to the village community. Land ceases to be a transferable commodity. The whole village community has the right of ownership over the land. The peasants are free to use land individually or collectively. Gramdan offers their equal opportunity to solve their problems mutually and amicably.

Gramdan has assumed greater significance as a programme for rural reconstruction and development. It provides all the opportunity to eradicate the class distinctions of haves and have-nots but creates a sense of service and sacrifice among the people. It makes the donors feel that their act of discarding ownership has been a step towards establishing peace and social justice. It certainly strengthens the society and improves the moral atmosphere of the village by way of mutual help and fellow feeling. While explaining the importance of Gramdan, Vinoba envisages the following five-fold programmes:-

(1) Creating an atmosphere of economic equality and liberty;

(2) Reviving the cultural life of the society by making the village a family;

(3) Discarding the land ownership concept, thus creating ethical atmosphere to settle disputes mutually without litigation, bad blood or bitterness;

(4) Establishing old *Varnashram Dharam* which is derivative of peace, fearlessness, compassion and faith.

(5) Protecting the society from outward aggression thus acting as a defence measure.

Gramdan indeed promises a revolutionary movement which seeks to create a new consciousness among the people and establish a new social order. The fundamental idea of Gramdan is everyman in the village should receive a plot of land to work upon. This will be achieved by doing away with the unequal distribution of land and by avoiding uneconomic holdings and unduly large holdings of land. The land distribution method may vary from village to village. All the land of a village can be pooled into one common; and distributed to each family for cultivation according to their need and strength to work. The individual will no longer be the owner of the land and the right of ownership will vest in the village community as a whole. The concept of Gramdan is a comprehensive one as it envisages to solve many problems at one and the same time e.g. (1) The problem of abolition of intermediaries no longer remains in a Gramdan village; (2) The problem of landless labourers is automatically solved; (3) The problem of land ceiling does not arise at all in a village after Gramdan; (4) The problem of co-operative or collective farming to which Gramdan movement is a practical approach is solved to a considerable extend; (5) It does away with uneconomic holdings and reduces the undue pressure of population on small plots of land; and (6) It incidentally does away with the subdivision and fragmentation of holdings.

The idea of Gramdan has wider implications. Vinoba regards it as a great solvent. It dilutes the forces of poverty and ignorance, disease and squalor and makes the accomplishment of big task of reconstruction of rural society easier. He evolved his own methodology of Gramdan. Vinoba says, "there should not be any landless in the village is my first step and the last is to see that there remains no land owner." Bhoodan provides land to the landless while Gramdan totally discards the idea of ownership. Bhoodan and Gramdan are inter-woven. While Bhoodan has the basis of compassion, the Gramdan has co-operation and equality. Hence Vinoba calls for Gramdan which regenerates society with its rich tradition of equity and social justice. Still Gramdan has something more to perform. Gramdan is not complete even if all the holders of land have pooled their holdings. Vinoba says that the landless labourers must also feel that they have pooled their resources with the landlords in the form of human labour. The wider implication of Gramdan is to surrender to the society whatever one has got for the benefit of his own self. It is like a promise of rendering unto Caesar the things which are Caesar's and unto God that are God's.

Gramdan therefore implies that the farmers should pool their labour and skill, tools and implements, their other resources of cultivation like animal power. They should also surrender their holdings of wells and tanks to irrigate the farms and make the same a common property of the village. Therefore all the individual belongings will be converted into the community goods and will belong to the village in common. Another thing, in the Gramdan village an individual is not entitled to sell or mortgage the land or lease or to dispose it off.

The principal idea the Gramdan movement is the abolition of private ownership of land. It creates the spirit of brotherhood and considerate feelings among the villagers and eradicates the differences between the villagers. All the problems concerning the village life should be solved collectively, thus it does not basically deviate from the original movement, but it is instead a manifest form of sprawling over the bounds the movement initially set up for itself.

Vinoba left it to the people regarding what are the agricultural pattern after Gramdan. But the general view is that all land would belong to the village in common and after distributing it according to the Gramdan method, one-twentieth portion thereof should be kept for landless labourers. But there is no fixed pattern of farming to be adopted by Gramdan villages. It may be individual, co-operative or collective. The people of the village are free to choose any type of farming. But the fundamental idea behind Gramdan is that one has to depend upon land for his livelihood must get land. The agriculturists may pool the whole land and cultivate it on co-operative basis

Vinobaji is in favour of such co-operative farming although he would not like to impose the pooling of the whole village land against the will of the people. Co-operative farming should be voluntary and not in the nature of an imposition. Vinoba is of the opinion that the productivity of land does not necessarily depend upon the size of the farm. In a country like India intensive methods of farming would be necessary. The plots should not be too small and the land should not be wasted by erecting boundaries between different fields. Villages should follow the Japanese method which adopts the following methods for cultivation:-

(1) Individual farming where every family has a separate plot;

(2) Co-operative farming where two or more families join together. It is like the joint-farming system adopted by the Government;

(3) Collective farming where whole village or a group of villages join together for cultivation.

In a nutshell, whatever be the pattern of cultivation, one thing is common in Gramdan that all work in a team spirit and a co-operative labour force is generated to tackle the problems of agriculture and rural reconstruction. This provides the basis of a socialized land economy in the village.

The Gramdan villages are organized on the lines of direct democracy. A direct method of democracy is being adopted through the formation of Gram Sabha. All the village activities are conducted through Gram Sabha which consists of all men and women. The Gram Sabha would meet from time to time to discuss all matters concerning the village development. The decisions should be unanimously or at least 3/4th majority. The main criteria is that most of the people should agree to it and give full co-operation to the Sabha. The constitutions may vary from village to village. The President and Secretary of Gram Sabhas are elected unanimously. To observe the day to day functions, there would be a working committee under the Sabha. The people can authorize the President of the Gram Sabha to constitute the working committee according to his own plan. Such Gram Sabha enjoys greater confidence of the people than the older form of Gram Sabha organized under the Panchayati Raj. In the Gram Sabha of Gramdan villages, unlike Panchayati Raj, people take personal interest and turn up in majority at the meetings to discuss the village industries, agricultural production, irrigational planning etc. The land revenue is collectively paid to the Government. Thus in Gramdan village, responsibility is shared by all. People offer their services directly for the progress of the village and develop their own personality.

There is a provision for the creation of a village fund (*Gram Kosh*) in every Gramdan village. The land holders have to offer one-fortieth off their production and the salaried people or wage-earners contribute one-thirtieth of their income annually. This village fund may be set up in the form of cash or grain or both. It provides a recurring income for the village which according to Gramdan rules, is spent on village welfare activities and on the disabled widows and sick people of the village. The Gramdan villages also establish labour co-operatives (Shramdan Samiti) to utilize the labour potentialities of the villages. People voluntarily offer labour, work on the fields educate children and develop the spirit of co-operation for the betterment of the society as a whole. The Gramdan village also has a shop of its own from where people purchase the things of their daily use. The trade and commerce of the village remains under the control of Gram Sabha. It estimates the needs of the people and tries to get things produced in the village itself. The Gram Sabha thus aims to reconstruct the economy of the village from the internal resources and make it self-sufficient in respect of food and agro-industrial products.

It was on 24th May, 1952, for the first time when the first Gramdan took place in Uttar Pradesh. It was the village named Mangroth in Hamirpur district, where all the holders of land denoted their entire land in Bhoodan and it was henceforward that Vinoba thought of complete Gramdan and started asking all the land-holders in a village to give up their holdings for the reconstruction of a new society in the villages. The idea thus was not based on any theoretical propositions but had come out from the natural and spontaneous activities of the people themselves. What Vinoba did was the induction of the law. Thus Gramdan became an economic principle, based on his reasoning and analysis of solving the rural problems and reconstructing its economy.

References

- Government of India, India 1966.
- M.L. Darling, The Punjab Peasant in Prosperity and Debt.
- G.C. Jangir, Indian Economy.
- R. Dutt and Sundharam, Indian Economy.
- Government of India, Agricultural Labour in India, Report on the Second Enquiry.
- Census of India, 1961.
- AIRCS General Report, Vol.II.
- S.S.S. Land Revolution in Orissa.
- The N.S.S. Report.
- Government of India, Report of the Panel of Land Reforms (1958).
- Bhowani Sen, Evolution of Agrarian Relations In India.

4

Progress of Bhoodan Movement

Vinoba's Bhoodan involves two processes i.e. Donation and Distribution. *Donation*: A procedure for donation has been laid down by the Madhya Pradesh Bhoodan Yajna Act of 1953. Any person desiring to donate land has to make a declaration of gift. The Bhoodan Mandal (Board) after accepting the gift forwards the declaration of donation to the Revenue Officer. The Revenue Officer, if satisfied that the donor is competent to make the gift and has a valid title in land, issues a notice to all those whom he considers to be interested in the donated land. If no objection is received within a specified time, the Revenue Officer accepts the gift on behalf of the Mandal. The gift has then to be registered under the Indian Registration Act of 1908. The registration is without any charge. A donation is rejected if the donor is incompetent to make a gift, if the title of the donor is defective, if there are encumbrances on the land or if there are any other reasons which the Revenue Officer thinks to be relevant for not accepting the gift. Even if the order has been passed by the Revenue Officer accepting the gift, any party aggrieved by the donation may reopen the case within a specified period by instituting a suit in a Civil Court. *Distribution:* After the process of donation are completed, the land is distributed by the Mandal or Tehsil Committees among the landless labourers. The landless labourers mean not only persons without any land but also persons possessing 2 acres of irrigated or 5 acres of un irrigated land. The persons among whom the land is distributed by the Mandal are designated as Bhoodan-lessees or Bhoodan-holders. Their right to hold the land is recorded in village papers or Record-of-Rights. A holder holds the land so long as it is vested in the Board. The leasehold right is heritable; but the holder is not allowed to transfer any interest in land to another person. He can not sublet the land, nor is he allowed to keep the land fallow for more than two years. If a Bhoodan-holder continues to hold a land for ten years without any breach of conditions laid down by the Board, he gets the same right in land as was held by the Board before the land was distributed. According to the Madhya Pradesh Bhoodan Yajna (Amendment) Act of 1964, a Bhoodan holder is deemed to hold the land direct from the State Government and is liable to pay the land revenue that may be assessed on his land. According to another amendment in the same Act, the Bhoodan-holder's land is not liable to attachment or sale in the execution of any decree or order passed by a Civil Court. The Board may also allot the donated lands for community purposes.

Initially there were in all 4,871 villages in Vidarbha in which 17,589 persons had donated 94,472.71 acres of land by 1969. The number of Bhoodan villages, the number of donors and the area initially donated in different districts is given in **Table 1**. The detailed information regarding

Table 1 : Number of Bhoodan Villages, and Area donated up to 1969 (District-wise)

District	Number of Bhoodan villages	Number of Donors	Area Donated (acres)
Akola	426	1177	7089.26
Amraoti	549	1461	5189.79
Bhandara	602	2062	4792.07
Buldana	198	421	2732.54
Chandrapur	577	1795	4984.15
Nagpur	672	1679	7396.28
Wardha	751	3770	12547.40
Yeotmal	1096	5219	49741.22
Vidarbha	**4871**	**17589**	**94472.71**

Table 2 : District-wise Donated Land for which Year-wise Information was Available

District	*Total Land Donated during 1951-1969 (acres)*	*Land for which year-wise information was available (acres)*
Akola	7089.26	1885.35
Amraoti	5189.79	614.71
Bhandara	2732.54	466.29
Buldana	4792.07	615.52
Chandrapur	4984.15	866.64
Nagpur	7396.28	973.94
Wardha	12547.40	2772.09
Yeotmal	49741.22	11876.32
Vidarbha	94472.71	20070.86

Table 3 : Year-wise Donation of Land in Different Districts

Year	Akola	Amraoti	Bhandara	Buldana	Chandrapur	Nagpur	Wardha	Yeotmal	Vidarbha
Up to 1952	-	40.93	-	-	-	13.52	139.52	3.00	196.97
1953	616.52	255.52	2.15	31.37	113.00	13.90	781.71	664.33	2365.55
1954	904.15	158.88	103.29	121.35	364.03	61.36	537.31	2201.34	4200.00
1955	126.25	67.42	28.09	172.66	339.24	577.41	855.14	4186.30	6378.30
1956	97.43	65.77	302.05	281.72	39.12	265.76	322.00	496.74	2170.71
1957	10.53	26.19	4.11	-	8.50	9.08	9.10	290.70	388.90
1958	-	-	-	1.65	-	10.00	1.03	119.14	140.32
1959	-	-	-	-	-	-	0.10	3741.26	3741.36
1960	-	-	-	-	1.75	-	4.05	27.10	31.15
1961	-	-	-	-	1.00	-	81.83	27.00	110.58
1962	-	-	-	-	-	22.91	33.47	55.65	113.03
1963	130.47	-	-	-	-	-	0.50	8.00	138.97
1964	-	-	-	6.77	-	-	5.33	40.24	52.34
1965	-	-	-	-	-	-	-	5.20	5.20
1966	-	-	26.60	-	-	-	-	10.20	36.80
1967	-	-	-	-	-	-	-	-	-
1968	-	-	-	-	-	-	-	-	-
1969	-	-	-	-	-	-	-	-	-
Total	**1885.35**	**614.71**	**466.29**	**615.52**	**866.64**	**973.94**	**2772.09**	**11876.32**	**20070.86**

the year-wise progress of donation in different districts is given in **Table 2** and **Table 3**. Out of the total initial donation as mentioned above, 22,860.68 acres were rejected by the State Government and hence 4,044 persons ceased to be donors and as a result of these ineffective donations as many as 852 villages virtually ceased to be Bhoodan villages. Thus the effective donation of land came to 68,359.76 acres. Total inhabited villages and net donation villages in different districts are mentioned at **Table 4**.

The total effective donation during 1951 to 1969 came to 68,359.76 acres, of which 48,902.72 acres were legally transferred by the Government to the Bhoodan Mandal by 1969 and 19,457.04 acres, though not legally transferred, were in the possession of the Bhoodan Mandal. Thus, both these areas (i.e. transferred and not-transferred) were available for distribution. **Table 5** shows year wise transfer of donated land by the Government to the Bhoodan Mandal in different districts.

Table 4 : Total Inhabited Villages and Net Donation Villages in Different Districts

District	Total Inhabited Villages	Net Donation Villages	Percentage of donation villages to total villages
Akola	1,508	272	18.04
Amraoti	1,609	419	26.41
Bhandara	1,486	515	34.66
Buldana	1,225	140	11.43
Yeotmal	1,629	961	58.99
Chandrapur	2,755	510	18.51
Nagpur	1,653	534	35.32
Wardha	972	618	63.58
Vidarbha	**12,837**	**4,019**	**31.31**

Table 5 : Year-wise Transfer of Donated Land by the Government to the Bhoodan Mandal in Different Districts

Year	Akola	Amraoti	Bhandara	Buldana	Chandrapur	Nagpur	Wardha	Yeotmal	Vidarbha
1951	-	-	-	-	-	-	-	-	-
1952	-	-	0.10	-	-	-	-	2.00	2.10
1953	-	1.00	9.03	5.76	-	-	46.35	1.00	63.14
1954	42.02	11.00	10.27	44.25	240.69	350.93	909.59	1471.06	3079.81
1955	645.69	1322.89	68.55	493.50	91.00	1583.46	913.75	8975.49	14094.33
1956	705.94	321.78	1734.21	291.38	711.77	826.17	1563.65	6891.55	13046.45
1957	910.82	269.88	153.40	74.10	1172.37	621.86	976.06	5208.46	9386.95
1958	104.15	30.83	205.08	197.20	77.82	12.00	299.88	2345.50	3272.46
1959	-	4.25	49.79	12.00	15.20	65.41	8.40	222.52	377.57
1960	-	0.31	30,00	-	-	48.89	-	2119.51	2198.71
1961	-	-	0.50	33.73	3.00	9.87	-	748.77	795.87
1962	-	-	74.19	40.00	-	10.23	-	381.81	506.23
1963	31.60	-	5.41	-	-	96.93	13.47	824.37	971.78
1964	8.60	46.10	1.00	-	-	21.40	8.00	425.20	510.30
1965	26.00	5.00	4.22	5.00	-	-	10.66	148.86	199.74
1966	27.90	-	10.32	-	-	-	-	284.52	322.74
1967	39.00	-	2.50	-	0.05	-	-	18.27	59.82
1968	-	-	1.30	9.42	-	-	1.0	2.0	13.72
1969	-	-	1.00	-	-	-	-	-	1.00
Total	**2541.72**	**2013.04**	**2360.87**	**1206.34**	**2311.90**	**3647.15**	**4750.81**	**30070.89**	**48902.72**
Percentage to Regional Total	**5.20**	**4.11**	**4.82**	**2.48**	**4.73**	**7.48**	**9.71**	**61.49**	**100.00**

After the Telangana Movement, Vinoba resumed his work of Kanchan-Mukti at the Paunar Ashram. During this time, Bhoodan had come to be widely known and many opinions were put forward both for and against it. When the news reached Pt. Nehru, he wanted to know Vinoba's views on land reforms and also his views on the Draft Report of the First Five Year Plan which was under preparation. For this purpose Pt. Nehru sent R.K. Patil, then Member of the Planning Commission to Paunar to discuss with Vinoba the draft outline of India's First Five Year Plan. Vinoba could not appreciate the plan, particularly the part which dealt with Khadi and Village Industries. For him, it seemed to be a total negation of the Gandhian spirit. Vinoba was highly critical in his approach and remarked: "I do not find just a mere ordinary difference between my and the Planning Commission's approach; it would not be possible to mend it only by erasing a few lines here or there. If you accept my views then the whole Plan will have to be revised". Vinoba also made it clear that the Plan was not consistent with the Directive Principles enshrined in the Indian Constitution particularly those regarding livelihood and work to all citizens. He said, "If you....can't provide work for all...you must resign...You as village industries to support themselves. You first cut off my legs and then want me to stand?"

The following are the classifications of Acharya Vinoba Bhave's pilgrimage for land:

1. *Pochampalli to Paunar*. Vinoba explained the concept of Bhoodan to his rural audience in a variety of ways. Vinoba accepted the land donations even from the poor. During his Padyatra from Pochampalli to Paunar which lasted around 51 days, he passed through

some 200 villages and received 12,200 acres of land for distribution among the landless.

2. *Paunar to Delhi*. Vinoba was in his mind that the idea of Bhoodan is a great solution of India's land problem and hence not only march up to Delhi alone but the decision was to cover the entire country. Vinoba covered nearly one hundred and eleven miles and collected about 2,000 acres of land with an average of 285 acres per day. This average was greater than the Telangana where he collected on an average of 200 acres per day. He reached the University town of Saugar on October 2, 1951. He remained in Madhya Pradesh for about25 days and collected nearly 6,400 acres from 563 donors. Then he encamped at Tikamgarh. Here the lands are mostly covered with forest and he had to walk across untrodden ways to deep woods to meet the people living in scattered villages. He toured the whole area for about five days and collected 800 acres of land from 204 donors. Vinoba once again went to Uttar Pradesh on October 16, and halted at Chirgaon. After several halts in Gwalior, Datia, Dambra and Dholpur he covered the districts of Agra, Mathura, Aligarh and Bulandshahar on his way to Delhi. By the time he reached Delhi on November 13, Vinoba received 19,436 acres of land in Bhoodan with an average of more than 206 acres per day.

Vinoba had covered from Paunar to Delhi about 792 miles with an average of sixteen to eighteen miles per day. He spent eleven days in Delhi and met the President, the Prime Minister, Members of the Planning Commission, Ambassadors, Press Reporters and several other social workers and leaders.

3. *Delhi to Sevapuri.* Vinoba left Delhi early in the morning of November 24, 1951 and marched towards Uttar Pradesh. He was having a revolutionary programme in his mind and thought Uttar Pradesh would provide him a comparatively better atmosphere to start with. Vinoba got favourable response from the people. During his stay at Mathura the constructive workers had decided to give their whole hearted support and co-operation to Vinoba's mission. They had fixed one crore acres of land as the final target and as the first installment thereof, they decided to collect five lakh acres of land within one year in the State. The burden of such a task was shouldered by Baba Raghavadas who joined this movement at the call of Vinoba. As a then MLA he showed great enthusiasm in solving the problems of the landless of Uttar Pradesh through the Bhoodan Mission. During his two years Padyatra of Uttar Pradesh, Baba Raghavadas received 38,900 acres of land from 6, 712 donors. He received Rs.46,199 as Sadhandan from 1,364 donors. He covered nearly 4,997 miles in Padyatra and halted at about590 villages of Uttar Pradesh. Vinoba has characteristically remarked that while the ambition was his, its fulfillment was of Baba Raghavadasji's.

Leaving Delhi, Vinoba first entered the district of Meerut on November 29, 1951. After covering almost all the districts of Western Uttar Pradesh he reached Sitapur on February 22, 1952. From Sitapur Vinoba reached Bahraich. From Bahraich he covered the districts of Gonda, Basti, Gorakhpur, Ghazipur and Ballia and then went to Banaras. Between Bahraich and Ballia he collected 17,476 acres at an average of over 400 acres daily. During this term, two important events happened, one is the Annual Conference of Sarvodaya Samaj and other is coming of Sri Jayaprakash Narayan. The Annual Conference of Sarvodaya Samaj was held from April 13 to 16, 1952 at Sevapuri, 14 miles west of Varanasi. It was attended by many great leaders and constructive workers of the country. Sri Krishnadas Jaju presided over this Conference which was inaugurated by Acharya J.B. Kripalani. Vinoba expounded before the Conference the ideology of Bhoodan and explained the revolutionary nature of the movement. He also explained in length with the concepts of Yajna, Dan and Tap in their economic contexts. Till this period, a total land of 1,02,362 acres from 4,936 donors were collected by Vinobaji. After Lucknow he went to Kanpur. Then he moved on Jalaun, Hairpur and Banda. In Hamirpur district Vinoba was given en entire village in donation. Diwan Shatrughan Singh, the biggest landowner of the area together with sixty five other families gave the entire village to Vinoba. When Vinoba moved to Banda

Town, he met Sri Jayaprakash Narayan. It was this meeting which turned J.P. the revolutionary into J.P. the reformer. Jayaprakash Narayan accepted Vinoba's ideology of the social change through non-violent action.

After covering the districts of Fatehpur, Raebariely, Sultanpur and Pratapgarh, Vinoba entered Allahabad in the last week of June, 1952. He received 27,561 acres of land from here. After Allababad he went to Mirzapur and then e-entered Varanasi on July 4, 1952. Thus the Bhoodan Yajna from September, 1951 to July, 1952 made an impressive progress. The average land received from Delhi to Sitapur was 314 acres. He had covered 3,750 miles and halted at 240 villages.

4. *Sevapuri to Bihar*. Vinoba's tour to Bihar was an experimental one. It offers a challenge to the social reformers and thinkers. Vinoba deliberately took the challenge in order to prove the potentialities of non-violent action for bringing about a change in the social and economic of the people. He entered Bihar on September 14, 1952 and stayed there for more than two years and started various programmes like Sampattidan, Shramdan and Jeewandan. Since Bihar was the home-land of Sri Jayaprakash Narayan, he also joined Vinoba in the Bhoodan movement. He started collecting land almost every day. From Patna Vinoba went to Gaya. Sri Damodardas with Sri Gauri Shanker Saran Singh formed a Committee to work out a plan. Vinoba was

forced to stay at Chandil for some months due to ill health till the Fifth Sarvodaya Sammelan held there on March 7, 8 and 9, 1953. In this Sammelan which was attended by nearly 2000 delegates from all over India, Vinoba placed a four-fold programme viz (i) integration of constructive work institutions; (ii) collection of 5 crore acres of land by the end of 1957; (iii) Sampattidan; and (iv) Yarn offering. Before this Sammelan, the people of Bihar contributed about 2,00,000 acres of land in Bhoodan. After the Conference, he resumed the padyatra. While he reached the district of Muzaffar, the whole area was seriously affected by heavy rains and floods. Vinoba placed a relief-programme. Thus Vinoba remained in Bihar for twenty seven months and visited five thousand villages. The total land collected in Bihar from September 14, 1952 to December 31, 1954 was 22,32,474 acres.

5. *Bihar to South India*. Vinoba first entered Orissa on January 26, 1955. In Orissa at Koraput, villages after villages were donated to him. His Orissa tour was completed on September 30, 1955 and he received 2,57,277 acres of land from 95,757 donors and 812 Gramdans. Then Vinoba entered Andhra Pradesh. During the course of his Padyatra there, he received 63,000 acres of land. Vinoba then reached Tamil Nadu on May 13, 1956. The Eighth Sarvodaya Sammelan was held at Kanchipuram. Crossing Chingleput District, he came to Pondicherry. During the

period from August to October, Vinoba remained in Coimbatore. Covering all most entire southern part of the country, Vinoba reached Kanya Kumari on April 1, 1957.

6. *Kanya Kumari to Kashmir.* From Kanya Kumari, crossing through the districts of Trivandrum, Quillon and Kottayam, Vinoba entered Trichur district and reached Kaladi on May 7, 1957. There he attended the Ninth All India Sarvodaya Sammelan. The Sammelan was presided over by Dada Dharmadhikari. In his Kerala tour, he received 1,571 acres of land and 301 villages in Gramdan. Leaving Kerala he entered Mysore State. In his presence at Yelwal, the decision regarding Purna Swaraj was taken and which was attended by the Prime Minister Pt. Nehru who gave his whole-hearted support to the Gramdan Movement. Then Vinoba went to Bombay and passing through Kolhapur reached Pandaripuram where he attended the Tenth Sarvodaya Sammelan in May, 1958. After this Vinoba reached Rajasthan and passing through Udaipur he reached Ajmer where he attended the Eleventh Sarvodaya Sammelan. After that he reached Kashmir through Rajpura, Chandigarh, Amritsar, Pathakot. During the summer of 1959, Vinoba remained in Kashmir and expounded the concepts of "*Shanti Sena*" and "*Jai Jagat*" or "World Peace". He called upon the forces of non-violence and truth to bring about social harmony and cultural unity among the people.

7. *Kashmir to Punjab.* After returning from Kashmir, Vinoba went to Amritsar on November 11, 1959. There he announced his decision to make a change in his Padyatra programme. The practice so far had been that his programmes were fixed for months in advance. Any change was difficult, therefore he decided to change to fix the programmes in a week advance so that more attention can be given on Bhoodan work.

8. *Punjab to Indore.* After his tour of Punjab, he proceeded to Indore via chambal valley are of Madhya Pradesh. The districts of Morena and Bhind of Madhya Pradesh have been notorius for robbery and dacoity for the last several decades. Since Vinoba had received various requests to visit the place, he planned to tour the area to propagate the philosophy of non-violence and to create a favourable atmosphere for voluntary surrender to the dacoits. Vinoba toured the Chambal Valley are for about a month. There were twenty dacoits surrendered before Vinoba and deposited their armaments. Later they were taken to judicial custody. After this, Vinoba moved on to Indore on July 24, 1960 and stayed there for one full month. During his stay there, he urged the people to create an atmosphere of purity so that life becomes virtuous and spirited.

9. *Indore to Assam.* During one of the meetings with Pt. Nehru, Vinoba was advised to visit Assam, the border State of India infested with many problems like communal riots,

languages differences, infiltration and tribal violence and unrest. So far Assam was the only State he was not visited. Vinoba entered Assam on March 5, 1961. He found Assam an "internally splitted" state with linguistic-cum-political rivalries. Vinoba appealed the people of Assam for Gramdan as that only could solve their problems. During his stay in Assam from March 5, 1962 to September 4, 1962, Vinoba received 500 Gramdans and 12,000 bighas of land in Bhoodan.

10. *Assam to Pakistan*. It was one of the most important developments of the Bhoodan Movement when Vinoba undertook the Padayatra of East Pakistan. Addressing the people of Pakistan, he requested to donate their lands for the welfare of the poor. In fact, on the very first day of his visit, he received land gift. Vinoba toured Pakistan from September 5, 1962 to September 20, 1962 and collected 176 bighas of land which was distributed on the same spot as was received, among forty-eight landless labourers.

11. *During Chinese and Pakistan Wars*. Vinoba's Bhoodan Movement was a process of revolutionary advance. He shifted the emphasis from Bhoodan to the new stage of Gramdan. Bhoodan will undoubtedly solve many problems of the landless but Gramdan would bring about a total transformation of the rural society; for unity and strength; for economic stability and justice; for security and service. On October 20, 1962 China

> attacked India. During this time, Vinoba suggested the formation of a permanent "defence line". To attain this end the people have to liquidate all their differences and come out to live as one community. Gramdan would bring about unity among the people. In times of danger – be it external aggression or internal conflicts – they must display their loving heart and a firm faith in collective living that go with Gramdan and Bhoodan – the Vinobian measures of defence and development.

The concept of Bhoodan originated in 1951. As the movement progressed, new phases of Sarvodaya came to light *Sampattidan* in 1952, *Shramdan* in 1953, and *Jeevanda*n in 1954. The Gramdan concept was added to the movement in 1955 which opened up the new vistas of *Gram Swaraj* in 1956. The concept of *Shanti Sena* in 1957, spread and sprawled over to one of world peace with its slogan of *Jai Jagat* in 1958. Slowly the concept broadened into one of all embracing word Sarvodaya in 1959, adding to it in 1960 the necessary accompanying idea of the non-violent conquest of violence. The "Defence Measure" aspect of it came to light during the Chinese and Pakistan Wars in 1962 and 1965 respectively. Up to March 31, 1967, Vinoba collected around 42,64,096 acres of land. It was a great achievement of the movement from the point of view of the millions of landless community of the country. The Planning Commission estimated to collect only twelve lakh acres of land for the landless after the enforcement of the Land Ceiling Acts in all the States of the country. Compared to this, the Bhoodan Movement has achieved a great success in collecting nearly four times of what Government would have collected by legislation. In addition, the Gramdan Movement provided new opportunities for re-building the village economy based on the principles of equality and justice where there would neither be a landless nor a landlord.

References

- Vinoba Bhave, Principles and Philosophy of the Bhoodan Yagna, 1976.
- Misra Raghavendra Nath, Bhoodan Movement in India: An Economic Assessment, 1972, Delhi.
- Suresh Ram, Towards a Total Revolution, 1968, Allahabad.
- Vinoba Bhave, Voice of Vinoba, 1955, Sarvodaya.

5

Ideology of Swaraj

Vinoba Bhave in his book Revolutionary Sarvodaya, narrates Sarvodaya as:-

> "Sarvodaya means that the good of all resides in the good of one. That there could be interests of one person, which are against the interests of another is inconceivable. Similarly, there could be no interests of one community, class or country which would be against the interests of any other community, class or country. *The idea of opposition of interests is itself wrong.*"

Vinoba had the logical status of a pre-supposition. It must be admitted that any notion of the natural disharmony of interests is, despite appearances, no more empirical than its opposite. If it is agreed that the existence or non existence of a particular God is beyond empirical proof, then a conception of a common "good of all" which predicated upon a conception of God would also be beyond the capacity of the scientific method to verify or disprove. It is therefore necessary to understand the thought of Vinoba Bhave is to realize that it represents the Indian idealistic tradition of the Vedanta. Vinoba while admitting having studied the works of Shankaracharya, a formulator of this tradition, "more than of any one else". He also agreed with him in holding that therein dwells in every man the same spirit. This spirit also called the soul or self, "is to be sought in our own hearts". But according to Shankaracharya, the same universal soul or Atman which informs all that is. It is in this context that Vinoba observed how "the beautiful atman within me is within the insect too." Vinoba's ideal of samya yoga, or reverence for all life, accordingly "makes no distinction between man and man" and even see "no ultimate difference in the spirit of man and other animals." Not only do all people "belong to one human family" by virtue of the one God being in each person, but all are viewed as but one manifestation of "that God (who) is present in all the forms of creation. However people are unique in that the human mind alone has the capacity to reflect upon being. It is a crucial prerogative of the mind to will attitudes which may either impede spiritual progress or overcome the illusion of separation which allows for final self-realization (moksha) to occur. It is to this end which Vinoba refers when he said that "the ultimate human good is not subjective, differing from individual to individual, it is uniform in nature." Religious conflicts are illusory. Vinoba recognised that "the growth of dogmas and rigid institutions around religions" has created much division, but nevertheless held that "all religions believe in love, compassion, affection and peace, and in this respect they have a common belief." Thus, "all religions are partial embodiments of Truth" or, to put it differently "Hinduism, Islam and other religions are different formulations of only one basic religion, namely,

Truth." Therefore the ethical content of a religion is its essence which "the highest goal of spiritual life lies in the ultimate experience....in which the worshipper.....is merged and becomes one with the infinite. Vinoba maintained, the essence of every religion is the same. Truth cannot oppose Truth and hence "there can never be opposition between two religions." Similarly Vinoba held that "the worth of a society is judged by its individuals" who constitute its essence. Since the essence or soul of each individual is the same, Truth that is Atman cannot oppose Truth, and again all conflict is illusion caused by "a false notion of what constitutes our interest". Since, a society is no more than the individuals who compose it, the "basic oneness of all life removes the possibility of conflict between the good of the individual and that of society." The concept of Sarvodaya comes to include the belief that "the good of the individual is contained in the good of all" as well as the conviction that the good of all is contained in the good of each individual. Those who do not believe in a "common good of all" but hold, rather, that the goal should be "the greater good for the greater number" Vinoba observed that "utilitarianism takes its utility for granted. It fails to be useful, according to him, when it comes to the ultimate goal of realizing the Oneness of all life. He even went further by asserting that utilitarian instrumentalities like a tradition of "majority rule" may even serve to inhibit the growth of this realization.

To others like Marx, who proceed upon the assumption of a conflict of self or class interests, Vinoba complained that such bases undermine "the very foundation of fellow feeling and mutual help". Indeed, so monistic was Vinoba's perspective that even the concept of the struggle for existence is "unjustified" as a denial of spiritual unity. Accordingly, while conflicts among individuals are born of ignorance of their common good, Vinoba believed that capitalism and competition, generally, impede the realization of this truth. Vinoba argued that "Capitalism cannot be ended by love or conflict, but by right thought." However, "right though" in this context is quite far from Marx's conception of consciousness because it is not dependent, in any way, upon one's material environments. "Right though" is dependent upon one's bhavana (mental attitude), which has "the power to transform all things." Indeed, in this context, "It is the eye of the beholder that determines the form of the world", not vice versa. Capitalism, in this sense, is caused like all "sources" of conflict, by a wrong attitude or perspective as to what is real in the world. He held that the source of all wrong attitude is taught to one by one's environment. This source is the bhavana that "I am the body" which "builds a wall around me and cuts me off" from others. He also observed how "from childhood we are taught to worship this deity, the body" and "we impress on the child's mind the idea that he is the body." This emphasizes the notion of "difference" upon the individual and builds a life "on the foundation of fear" which is conducive to selfishness and conflict. According to Bhave "obsession with the flesh is the source of all fear" and "it is because of fear that tyranny becomes possible." When people fall into "the whirlpool of beautifying the body" and seek only to gratify their sensual desires and whims, naturally conflicts arise and the most physically strong and mentally clever will exploit others for their own ends. Those others, more often that not, will endure the exploitation because of the fear they hold with regard to asserting themselves. How to overcome this fear? According to Vinoba, to progress to a realization of the oneness of all life is to understand the truth of the Bhagavad-Gita's thirteenth chapter : "Tat tvam asi" means "You are indeed the self; you are not the body, you are the self". As interpreted by Vinoba this means that the Self or Atman in every person is "altogether distinct from the body, separate, entirely beautiful, bright, holy and free of imperfection." It is in sort "indestructible, flawless, transcending the body" and, hence, worthy to be exalted. The revolutionary flavor of this perspective may become more apparent as no true safety is possible so long as there is attachment to the body and consequent fear. The possibility of "real freedom" in either a spiritual or political sense, moreover, presupposes a conquering of fear. When one gives up attachment to the body, he becomes an emperor and achieves freedom. "True safety" and "real freedom" in this context consist in willfully surrendering to the Self who then "guides us all from within". In a word, they consist in attaining to the ideal of moksha. Thus, while God has given us freedom to identify ourselves with the body, God has also given the mind the capacity to will a new bhavana by which attachment to the body may be transcended. To be truly free and safe in either a spiritual or political sense, therefore, requires that we progressively realize that "common good" which is moksha and individually admit that "I am the Self." It is the extent to which this bhavana is mastered, according Vinoba, that each individual" is then emperor of the world." However, this ought not to be taken to mean that the body should be mortified in any way. While one must, according to Vinoba, see that "I am not this mortal body.... I am the spirit that never dies." One must also realize that "the body has been given to me for the sake of the Self." "The body is like one's clothes" or a "machine" which should be well used as an :"instrument" in the service of God's will. It needs to be treated well in other words, since it is a prerequisite for doing one's duty.

According to Hindu tradition, "everybody has a duty to fulfill." In fact, the very start of the teachings of the

Gita is based on the principle that whatever might be the position in which a man is placed at birth, if he performs his duty with love, devotion, and singleness of purpose, he becomes worthy of moksha (self-realization). This duty or svadharam, consists of two parts according to Vinoba : the dharma, which changes, and the "natural duties" which never change. To interpret dharma as changeable is highly revolutionary in the context of the traditional caste system. That system holds that "One's dharma consists in following one's true vocation." which is by nature that which one is born into. Vinoba held however that "the idea of associating birth in poverty or prosperity with previous life is totally absurd." For Vinoba, true vocation is thrown open to change as he argued that "as the course of one's life changes through thinking and experience, one's old dharma drops off and a new dharma comes in its place." There are however duties which are natural and unchanging, for example : "The service of the parents to whom I was born, the service of the neighbours amongst whom I find myself, these duties come to me naturally....my other obligations are matters of everyday experience. I feel hungry, I feel thirsty. So, to give food to the hungry and drink to the thirsty becomes my duty by nature. The criterion which is employed in the science of ethics for determining whether from the point of view of morals a principle is right or wrong, and whether from a practical point of view it is advantageous or disadvantageous is to extend it to apply to all people and see what the result is. Since the body is given to us as a means, an instrument" to be used in God's service, and since the instrument needs to be well cared for to be of full service, to be denied basic bodily needs is an impediment to doing one's svadharma. Vinoba's admiration "to foster and cherish the body because only so can one perform one's svadharma" linked with an imperative to "do unto others as you would have them do unto you", thus, at least, means that in so far as one has more than one needs for physical well being, one's duty is to "give food to the hungry and drink to the thirsty". Although "physical well being" admittedly has different needs from individual to individual, still "the body is to be paid its due hire – no more than that" or one will tend to fall back into the spirit-denying "I am the body" or one will tend to fall back into the spirit-denying "I am the body" bhavana. Clearly this would seem to be the basis from which Mira Behn, another disciple of Gandhiji, criticized Vinoba's occasional acceptance of land gifts from the very poor : such gifts do not allow the giver's body its "due hire". During the Bhoodan Movement, Vinoba observed that "the first step to bring about Sarvodaya is Antyodaya – the uplift of the last one" Accordingly, he taught that "it is also the duty of the poor kisan to give" because, from the point of view of the landless, he is somewhat better off." This Vinoba argued would "give rise to a moral power that would affect the rich" something which he saw actually happen on many occasions. He says :...everybody must make some sacrifice for the sake of those who are the most distressed in society even as all water of the globe flows towards the sea standing at the lowest level. As can be seen clearly, as the see level rises, the poorer people who once gave more than they could afford would be subsumed in the giving. Thus while Vinoba might depart from the rationale of Mira Behn until a basic subsistence level is established for all, that rationale might well be used by Vinoba to support his call for all to perform their svadharma. In the meantime even the poor would have an opportunity to discover that each person "experiences joy and fulfillment in the measure which he gives."

Vinoba held that because human nature is social, no person can partake of any good thing alone and find happiness. Proceeding from his metaphysical premise that "in reality it is impossible to separate the individual and society." The prevailing values in a society as having a basis in the consensus of the people in that society. By mobilizing even the poor to adopt a new value orientation the status conferred upon the rich by the old order is undermined. "moral pressure" is thus exerted with the aim of giving "the opportunity to the rich to give vent to their generous nature." It is not that people are simply good by nature. For Vinoba "none but God is wholly free from blemish...none too is an embodiment of absolute evil." Of course, that God who "dwells in the hearts of all beings" is by definition, good. Still, while "the natural movement of one's soul is upwards" it is believed that "the burden of the body drags down the soul" Human beings, accordingly, have the potential for evil as well as goodness in so far as the mind dwells upon the selfish comforts of the body. Indeed there are many external forms assumed by the illusion that strews with thorns the path of *svadharma*. Yet, if we examine them, only one thing is at the bottom of it all, namely a restricted and shallow identification of oneself with the body. In his point of view, "change always goes on" because the attractions of the body and the desire of the soul to realize itself are in a constant tension. It is in this context that Vinoba observed how "the Gita uses the allegory of war" and maintains that "to speak the truth, the real battle is only within ourselves." Full self-realisation (*moksha*) hence becomes an ideal to be approached as one progressively abandons the bhavana of "I am the body". Therefore he observed that we should control over all our senses, mind and hearth. We refuse to be slave of them. Whence our Vedic rishis gave as the mantra "*Yatemmahi Swarajya*" (we shall strive to attain this Swaraj). In this context, individual swaraj (self-rule) becomes, a prerequisite to moksha Rule of the Self over the body is attained as the mind is able to separate the two in one's consciousness. To enable to do this, he agreed with the orthodox Hindus, one must successfully overcome the "three gunas". These qualities of nature are assumed present in all forms of life and were for ambition (*rajas*) and knowledge (*sattva*). They may also be conceived of as being represented in one's instincts, emotions, and intellect, respectively. Experience shows that just as the mind is influenced by bodily sickness, so also good health has a bearing on mind." Tamas is accordingly overcome by the performance of bodily labour. This cure, moreover, has social significance in so far as Vinoba applied his categorical imperative – extending this individual good to all members of the society. Seeing how many people are entrapped by tamas due to their exploitation of the labour of others. He even argued that it is in the spiritual interest of the rich to work with their own hands. He asserted : all inequality, all ideas of high and low, slavery and violence have originated chiefly from the economic sin of avoiding bodily labour. Thus as one identifies oneself with the body, so also one may extend that identification to building up a corporation or a large plantation which one considers "necessary" in order not to work. Such economic walls also are in conflict with Vinoba's desire to establish a "welfare of all" consciousness. If one has not overcome rajas, one will be subject to emotional judgement generally, and personal ego, fulfillment in particular. Where the identification with an illusory individual ego is not strong, there will be "unsteadiness" or purpose. Where the ego is strong, one is predicted to either over-extend one self in one's activities, so as to do little well (a violation of *dharma*) or, in the very least, one will perpetuate one's bhavana of "separateness" which is of course a spiritual barrier.

The major step to take in the effort of destroy the rajasic element is living within the limits of svadharma. So we must confine our actions and service to our's most immediate surrounding first. After our parents and neighbours are well taken care of, svadharma's sphere is allowed to legitimately grow. Such a focus on the 'nearest' is considered to be good combat against the ego's belief in its own capacity to 'change the world". Humility is fostered. In addition, the crucial importance of the results of our actions for both the tamas and rajas – dominated individuals. Vinoba narrated how :

> "The attitude that I perform any act, I must also enjoy its fruit, illustrates the dominance of the Rajasic-element. On the other hand, the attitude that if I have to give up the fruit, I shall refrain from all action itself, betrays a Tamas-dominated nature."

Main basis for such attachment to the fruits of one's actions is egoism – the sense of one's separateness from others. Thus egoism must be conquered first before one can seek freedom from attachment. "Egoism is conquered by constancy in sattva. The intellect, or reason, the faculty which allows us to accumulate knowledge, unlike "*rajas and tamas*" should be wounded, but not killed" since it is conceived as the way by which we may discover how similar we are to other being and how little, as individuals, we can do in this world. Also involved in this "constancy in sattva" is the removing of our identification with our mind which was, to transcend our attachment to it.

Vinoba says "One way to achieve victory over sattva, and hence, over egoism is to so live that "sattva becomes so much our nature that we would cease to be proud of it." The ways to God realization of *jnana* and *raja yoga*, through knowledge and psychological exercises respectively are paths suited for only a few temperaments. For the masses of humanity, however, sattva may be overcome only as "attachment is conquered by giving up the desire for results, and dedicating all to the Lord. Hence our reliance is solely on Him to Whom we have dedicated our life. This is the path of devotion or Bhakti. While Vinoba held that individual Swaraj can be achieved by "straight and simple bhakti", the key to understand the political relevance of this is to realize that the object of the loving devotion is not some historical incarnation or other abstract principle or entity, but mankind today, Vinoba's bhavana of bhakti teaches that "one should look upon all men and women as so many images of God." Since, for Vinoba, "Brahmin meant any lofty exalted idea" pertaining to life, "Society" became, for him, worthy of the devotion of individuals. Directing one's loving devotion, or bhakti, to Society is of course, consistent with Vinoba's Advaita Vedanta framework. Earlier it was noted how, according to this framework, there is no real conflict between individuals and society. Later it was discovered that the sense of attachment to the fruits of one's actions, and hence the gunas, could only be overcome "dedicating all to the Lord." Therefore, Vinoba Bhave combined the orthodox maxim that "renunciation of fruit is yoga, the art of living" with his own objective of renunciation of private ownership to God, or Society, as a means of land redistribution. According to Vinoba:

> "A psychological change like this cannot be brought about by war and violent revolution. It can only be brought about by the methods of Buddha, Christ, Ramanuja and other great teachers. Ultimately, it is to be the dedication of one's all for the well-being of all."

Indeed, the means of love and individual Swaraj may be conceived of as insparable components of the need which, if fostered by the mind's bhavana shall grow into the tree of moksha. Thus "the individual 'ego' can be dedicated to God only after it has been merged in the collective 'ego' and this latter can be accomplished only through progressive identification with the loving devotion to all that lives. Even for the materially oppressed, therefore, "to resort to cruelty for freeing oneself from the blame of cowardly behavior is like flying from the frying pan into the fire. For the non-Vedanta, Vinoba argued that non-violence or love, is not only intrinsically good but is also practical from an instrumental perspective. Speaking broadly Vinoba observed that:

".....the Communists consider everyone among the rich as an enemy of the poor. This attitude (*bhavana*) makes the good as well as the bad among the rich join together with the result that the wicked among them gain more strength. Class warfare, moreover, is "a process of revolution based on violence, is verily a process of reaction which can only result in counter revolution" for at least two reasons. First, it alienates potential allies within the opponent's class whose physical destruction is a loss of a well-educated and entrepreneurial resource who, as trustees, could be of great service to society. Secondly, if we want a concern for human life to be increased, or, ideally, for even our opponent to improve in this regard, "we cannot do so by the use of physical force, which only heightens the body sense". By threatening another's life, we destroy any consciousness that person has of existing oneness and remove the small possibility of rational communication since the atmosphere is charged with fear. He further maintained that "what the world appears to us to be depending on the vision we have of it." Therefore, the bhavana (mental attitude) that another individual or class or people are 'enemies' tends to make them appear to be enemies because that is what we draw out of them. Treated like enemies they usually act like enemies, thus reaffirming the bhavana. He further advocated, in his bhavana of bhakti, was to refuse to act like an enemy even if an opponent considers one as such.

This bhavana can make "the undeserving deserving and the evil good" since, through non-retaliation, the conception of one as a threatening "enemy" is difficult to sustain. Moreover, it encourages communication and the seeking of Truth (which no one is again completely without) by refraining from a self-righteous or absolute judgement. Hence Vinoba said:

> "Who is to decide that anyone is bad? Even if a really bad person appears before you, think that it is the Lord Himself. Even a villain will become a saint. The body perished every moment, understanding this, let us use it for the sake of svadharma. When there is need, let us not hesitate even to give it up for the sake of svadharma. Whenever there is a chance of the Supreme principle being defiled...I shall ever be ready to offer up the body in sacrifice in order to keep the flame of the Self brightly burning."

Therefore, to attain perfect individual Swaraj or self-realization requires one to be perfectly loving, Vinoba nevertheless held that "there is nothing impossible for the soul" and that "thought-force has no limitations." The objective that "my ego should completely get destroyed" is attainable if, at the point of death, one is so unattached to one's body as to dedicate all to the Lord, the Atman. To be so loving has, as an ideal, that of Jesus who is quoted by Vinoba as saying "They will be done, Lord, forgive them for they know not what they do." He believed that "Bhakti yoga must be coupled with karma yoga." Bhakti, or loving devotion is "the disposition to serve" while karma, or action, is the actual service." Accordingly, "the outer form of love is service" which is activity that is never renounced. Indeed, Vinoba held that "to renounce action is impossible for renunciation itself is an act." What is abandoned, ideally, is the sense of an ego either initiating action or enjoying the fruits thereof. It becomes such a tool not only as the bhavana of bhakti is developed within the individual's mind but also in so far as the bhakti is manifested in active service to others. Thus, we are told that "a devotee of God relishes karma yoga, the philosophy of action with non attachment" because that action is seen as "a form of worship." This has an opportunity to serve the people, moreover helps one to learn "to see God in every living being". Thus in the sense of karma yoga, one is better able to see why there are "unchanging duties" also included in one's svadharma. The individual seeker after Swaraj, therefore, is dependent upon the existence of others to be of service to. All persons within a society, then are viewed as individuals who are interdependent upon the same God within each, so to speak. In this context, Vinoba observed that 'we are from the beginning debtors" and how "discharge of the debt is yajna or service not altruism". Indeed "we have to beware of altruism" not only because it fosters identification with one's ego but also because it tends to deny, that "as we are born, our svadharma is also born with us". The *karma yogin*, therefore, in addition to performing service for its own sake as a means of "spiritual development" also acts out of a sense of duty to the society to which a great debt is owed. The general formulation of "the Lord to serve, I the servant, and creation the means" becomes, less personal as the ego is subordinated to "the Lord". Ideally, the individual *karma yogin* so transcends individual selfishness as to adhere merely to the maxim of "service to an individual and devotion to the whole society". Individual Swaraj is thus attained to as one sees that "in truth, *svartha* should be *paramartha*, one's own good should be the supreme good" and one identifies "with the community....around one."

Some of the complexity of the relationship between

the Swaraj (self rule) of individual and collective swaraj may be appreciated. While true collective Swaraj as alluded is literally the Sarvodaya ideal of *Ram Rajya* (the Kingdom of God). It would be unfair to conceive of its approximation as merely the sum of swaraj individuals have attained to. Just as the individual in society is dependent upon others for the fruitful practice of karma yoga in a spirit of bhakti, so also are those others dependent upon the renunciate's actions for such service as one may offer. The bhavana of "I am the body" was recognised to be more likely as the body's needs are not met. The actions of the karma yogin, become truly of service only in so far as they are conducive to the self of others being realized by them. Accordingly the activity of Vinoba's seeker after Truth is dedicated to providing the material necessities of life to others beginning with those who are in most need. A dialectic of sorts is thus established with both the served and the serving benefiting spiritually. Vinoba admitted that he grew from his youthful days to gain a greater concern for collective Swaraj. This prompted him, like Gandhiji to conduct expanded experiments of collective action as represented in the Bhoodan and Gramdan Movements. Vinoba hoped to create 'swatantra loka shakti' or 'the self reliant power of the people' by organizing individuals and promulgating the ideal of karma yoga on a mass scale. This 'power of the people' when manifested in different levels of society gave rise to another usage of "swaraj". Thus as Vinoba used the term "National Swaraj" was attained when independence was won from the British but "Gram Swaraj" or village self-rule has not yet been attained. Progressively, as the individual participates in the movement for national independence, then for regional autonomy and then for village self-reliance. Karma Yoga is "the way to God through right action" is only effective if the "right action" is "right", that is, as the bhavana of bhakti is manifested in it. Thus the "power of the people" was, a power which is "opposed to violence" or even asserting "pressure by the threat of violence.". It is based upon "the strength of good public opinion" which, when exerted, always respects the life and integrity of the opponent. However, when it comes to comparing the swatantra loka shakti with the power of the State which has as its base "the coercive power of law" Vinoba observed that "though there is no direct opposite", still "the two are qualitatively different".

References

❑ Sen Bandhudas, Bhoodan Movement, 1952.

❑ Publications Division, Acharya Vinoba Bhave, 1955.

❑ Vinoba Bhave, From Bhoodan to Gramdan, 1957, Tanjore.

❑ Vinoba Bhave, Principles and philosophy of the Bhoodan Yagna, Sarvodaya.

6

Agrarian Economy

Vinoba started the Bhoodan Movement not for mere a charity but the basic aim of this is to rejuvenate the rural economy. Most of the Indians are below poverty and ignorance and there is an emergent need of social and economic development of people. Vinoba's Bhoodan Movement offers good opportunity to the village people in making them so conscious of their economic and social rights and responsibilities. Since land is the basic source of production in the villages, its mal-distribution has created many problems. According to the Estimates for 1964-65, out of a net national income of Rs.20,100 crores, about 51.3 per cent i.e. Rs.10,270 crores was contributed by agriculture alone. Despite of the growing population on land, the agricultural sector continues to occupy a prominent position in the national economy. The Census, 1961 reveals, 82 per cent of the people live in villages and the agriculture remains the largest single occupation.

Even though the independence brought some drastic spectacular changes in the country's economy, the old economic condition remained almost unchanged so far as the agricultural productivity and the increasing shortage of food grains are concerned. After the First Five Year Plan the prices of food grains took an upward turn and by the year end of 1959, the food problem had become acute and assumed grave proportions. The Third Five Year Plan also witnessed rise in the prices of food grains.

The another factor which affects society very considerably was the occupational structure. The ratio of Primary, Secondary and the Tertiary occupations indicate levels of economic development. Agriculture, Manufacturing and Transport industries are grouped to govern the nation's economy. The ideal combination of these occupations depend upon the size, nature and potentialities of those factors. The Indian economy is occupationally agricultural. This agrarian structure of the country is responsible for the tardy growth of Indian economy. Indian Economy at this juncture needs an overall changes - a total transformation of the rural sector. The problem is thus of "lifting agriculture from its low equilibrium and braking the mesh of inter-locking factors such as out-dated technique, primary poverty and low productivity which tend to pull it downward." For achieving the desired aim and result, there must be an improvement in the economic condition of the agricultural labour and the cultivator which is the backbone of the rural economy of India.

As per 1961 Census, out of 131 million agricultural workers, 99.5 million were cultivators and 31.5 million were agricultural labourers. Thus agricultural workers formed about 70 per cent of the total working force for India. Taking the country as a whole, out of every 6 workers, 1 is agricultural labour. In Assam and Rajasthan, out of every 100 workers, there are 4 agricultural labourers as against 29 in Andhra Pradesh, 23 in Bihar, 21 in Maharashtra and Gujarat, 18 in Madras, 17 each in Kerala, Orissa and Madhya Pradesh and 16 in Mysore. In West Bengal and Uttar Pradesh there are 15 and 11 agricultural labourers respectively for every 100 workers.

The first important category is the 'Cultivator'. The term "Cultivator" includes all type of workers engaged in agriculture (other than wage earners). Briefly it means the person who earns his/her major income from land but does not earn wages by offering labour on the land of others. A cultivator may or may not own land or may cultivate the land himself or get the land cultivated by others. He must exercise his decision. In the 1951 Census, the cultivators had been classified as (i) cultivators of land wholly or mainly owned and their dependents; and (ii) cultivators of land wholly or mainly un-owned and their dependents. According to 1961 Census, the category of cultivators covers both owner and tenant cultivators. Cultivation includes ploughing, sowing and harvesting but does not include fruit growing or keeping orchards or groves or working for plantation... Besides actual cultivation involving manual work, persons engaged in active supervision or direction of cultivation are included in this category. The dependency concept of 1951 Census has been dropped. Thus in the 1961 Census, two subgroups of cultivators viz. cultivating owners and non-owners had been recognised. Another classification is that of rentiers. The 1951 Census had named them as non-cultivating owners of land. However the 1961 Census dropped this category mainly due to the reason that the laws concerning Zamindari abolition came in to force in all the States.

The other important category is that of the "Agricultural Labourers". They are those, whose business merely is to perform physical labour in the manner required by the cultivators. They do not take any risk and responsibility of cultivation. According to 1961 Census, "an agricultural labour" is one who works on another person's land without exercising any supervision or direction in cultivation for wages in money, kind or share of production. He has no right or lease or contract on land on which he works." According to Second Agricultural Labour Enquiry Report, the non-agricultural occupations performed by him are (i) Farming; (ii) Dairy Farming; (iii) Production, Cultivation and Harvesting of any commodity; (iv) Raising of live-stock, bees or poultry; and (v) Any practice performed on a farm as incidental to or in conjunction with the farm operations.

The "Agricultural Labourers" had been classified in to two groups namely (i) Attached; and (ii) Casual. An attached labour is one who works under continuous employment contract An attached labourer is one who works under continuous employment contract with the landlord, seasonally or annually, with or without "debt-bondage" or with or without "tie-in-allotment" of land. Different recruitment and retention methods are followed. Their terms and conditions of employment differs from region to region according to tradition and custom. A casual labourer is one who works without continuous employment on daily wages for specific agricultural operations which last only for a short duration. They are paid marketing rates and remain free to seek alternative employment if they so choose. They are however employed from time to time according to the exigencies of work. The above classification carries the workers being "free" and "unfree" or "bound". The workers have to render customary services such as household work and other non-agricultural services as desired by the employer. The agricultural labourers suffer mostly from the social and economic disabilities and are prone to exploitation. The work period of an attached labourer is usually longer than that of the casual labourer. The quantum differs from place to place.

The major part of the income of agricultural labour is derived from wages. They have generally no other occupations of their own. The paucity of resources and lack of enterprise are the main reasons which come in the way of their self-employment or alternative occupations. The study of wage rates and the mode of their payment reveals the deteriorating condition of the agricultural labour in India. Industrial wages are too high. The evil of irregularity of payment is also widespread. The average daily wage rate has gone down.

Land is the basic source of production. To a socialist, land is the property of the State and all activities concerning land use and production are controlled by the State. To a capitalist, land is a marketable commodity and whosoever owns it has full authority over its use and organisation. However to one who is having faith in human values, land is as free a gift of nature as air, water and sun. To such a person, land is a free source of production and must be shared equally by all. To a Sarvodaya philosopher and a critic of private property like Vinoba, the ownership of land is the main cause of economic disparities among the agriculturists. Vinoba says "Land is neither yours nor mine; it is God's who made it. Discard your pretensions of ownership. God created everything. How can you claim ownership on the strength of a lot of papers you have?" With such a diverse views on land ownership and management, one has to find out a satisfactory basis for land reforms. In India the main purpose of land reforms has been to remove the vestiges of an outdated system that had prevailed since long and had tended to cripple the agrarian economy. The objective thus was to "allow the land service of the country to function closer to the interests of the cultivators." It was to bring the actual cultivator into direct relationship with the State." The land policy adopted in the First Plan was to encourage the tiller of the soil by sanctioning him the right of ownership of the land which he cultivated and thus allowing him to reap the benefit of the labour he put on it.

Tenancy Reforms relate to regulation of rent, security of tenure and confirmation of ownership of tenants. Formerly there were two systems namely "Intermediary Estates" and "Raiyatwari Holdings" prevalent. The intermediaries were not always cultivating their home farm lands. Even the tenants holding land under intermediaries were not in all cases cultivating their land and were in turn creating "sub-tenancies". Since the tenants had not enjoyed protection under the right of permanent and heritable possession, legislative activity in this sphere was recently directed to protecting their rights. The security of the tenant, for instance, was subjected to the landlord's right to resume some area of land for personal cultivation. In the absence of personal cultivation, the landlords were able to resume land from tenants and get them cultivated by hired labour, crop-sharers or disguised tenants. After independence, intermediaries had been removed. In spite of the abolition, the big landlord magnets still dominate the rural economy. Feudalism still lives not only in the minds of the agriculturists, both rich and poor, but also in the facts of our agrarian structure. Disparities are still very wide and make our political democracy in the villages devoid of economic and social content.

It had been noticed that about 25 per cent of big landholders occupy more than 70 per cent of the operated area. The majority of the rural households is composed of small land-holders and 28 per cent of the rural households are reported to be landless. In order to remove this disparity, legislation putting ceiling on future as well as on existing holdings, has been enacted by almost all the States. The objectives behind this as indicated by the Panel of Land Reforms, are to reduce glaring inequalities in land ownership and income and to enlarge the sphere of self-employment. Even though some changes have been brought about the legislation in the rural economy, land reforms could succeed only to a limited extent. The main objectives viz. "to remove such impediments upon agricultural production as arise from the character of the agrarian structure"; and, "to create condition for evolving as speedily as may be possible, an agrarian economy with high levels of efficiency and productivity" have been largely defeated. The growing number of agricultural workers, the increasing number of the landless rural households and the prevailing practice of 'hired labour', all are characteristics of an agrarian structure more of a capitalistic form than that conforming to a "socialistic pattern."

The important feature of such an economy is the preponderance of tiny plots or land. There are 49.2 million operational holdings, possessing in an area of 326.2 million acres of land in rural India, the average size being 6.63 acres. Each operational holding on an average is constituted by 5.82 fragments and the average size of each fragment is only 1.14 acres. In addition, there is no strict regularism or security of tenure. "The law provides that all leases must be registered and in case of non registered leases, land will — in the person actually occupying it. But 'still a back door has been opened through non-recognition of share-cropping and sub-letting...."

Vinoba's quest, is therefore, to establish Lok-Shakti (Civil Power) by creating a sense of responsibility and dignity in the minds of the people so that they might come forward as an organised force and win over the forces of economic disruption and social disintegration. Only the power of people can bring about a new change in the social outlook and economic behaviour. Vinoba says that the force behind the Bhoodan Movement is based on 'Jan-Shakti' as opposed to 'Dand-Shakti' or 'Himsa-Shakti'. He launched this movement purely for people and established personal contacts with millions of them living in the country, teaching them the message of love and sacrifice so that they might come up with a bold step to rejuvenate the rural life. He first started with land. But his Bhoodan Movement is not confined to land alone. He has gained long strides in advancing the philosophy of Shramdan and Sampattidan which means offering of labur, wealth and other resources for the good of the society. Concentrating on the problem of village economy and land distribution, Vinoba has pleaded that all land belongs to God and that it should be shared equally by everybody. Vinoba views a "four-tier" classification among the people of India from the economic point of view. At the top are the big landlords possessing more than 100 acres of land and cultivating through hired labour and disguised tenants. Next comes the self-cultivators with 20 or more acres of land who maintain life with or without hired labour. Then comes those small peasants who maintain only a tiny plot of land and do their own cultivation without hired labour and lead a very hard life. At the bottom comes the landless who work as the cultivating labourers who are classified as attached and casual workers. They remain very poor and can scarcely manage two meals a day. Vinoba has named these groups as *Dhani* (Big Landholders), *Sukhia* (Rich Peasants), *Dukhia* (Small Cultivators) and *Bhukhia* (the Landless). The Second Agricultural Labour Enquiry Report has also classified these agriculturists as (A) Big Land

Owners; (B) Land-Owners-cum-Tenants; (C) Landless Tenants; and (D) Agricultural Labourers. Grouping (C) and (D), the ratio roughly comes as : A:(B:C):D = 2: 78.3 : 19.7. The National Sample Survey of 16th round of the year 1960-1961 had estimated the percentage of the landless (Class D) as 28. It even indicated that the number of the landless had increased by 8.3 percent.

The Bhoodan Movement always maintained that there should be no landless in the village and the Gramdan Movement has an ideal that there should be no land owner in the village. Briefly Bhoodan is the starting point whereas Gramdan is its consummation. Vinoba evolved a technique of mass contact and successfully displayed the efficacy of sour-force as against the coercive and violent force in establishing Gram Swaraj. His method was non-violent and peaceful and his approach was dynamic and all-comprehensive. Vinoba's technique of asking land from every group of the land owners was based on the principle of economic justice and social affection. Thus Vinoba offered a great solution to the problems of rural economy in the shape of the Bhoodan and the Gramdan Movements.

References

- ❑ Vinoba Bhave, Revolutionary Sarvodaya (Bombay : Bharatiya Vidya Bhawan, 1964).
- ❑ Vinoba Bhave, Democratic Values and the Practice of Citizenship (Kashi : Sarva Seva Sangh Prakashan, 1962).
- ❑ Indu Tikekar, Integral Revolution : An Analytical Study of Gandhian Thought (Varanasi : Sarva Seva Sangh Prakashan, 1970).
- ❑ Vinoba Bhave, Talks on Gita (Varanasi : Sarva Seva Sangh Prakashan, 1970).

- Vinoba Bhave, Random Reflections (Varanasi : Sarva Seva Sangh Prakashan, 1971).
- Vinoba, Random Reflections.
- Vinoba Bhave, Democratic Values.
- Vinoba Bhave, Sarvodaya and Communism (Tanjore Sarvodaya Prachuralaya, 1957).
- Vinoba, Gramdan for Gramswaraj.
- Huston Smith, The Religions of Man.
- Vinoba, Bhoodan Yagna.

7

Comments on Democracy

> "The Sarvodaya Movement believes in the supreme importance of the individual. The ultimate goal of all evolution is the full flowering of his....creative autonomy. It is only self-knowledge that makes the uniqueness and autonomy not a threat to the world but its most cherished asset."

The individual is "supremely important" because the spiritual search for truth, for Parama Samya which is the "ultimate reality" of God, could only be conducted by individuals. "Collective Swaraj" while capable of being approached in an organised fashion, is based upon the actions of individuals practicing karma yoga in a bhavana of bhakti. Thus the "self-knowledge" is attained to involve the "full flowering of one's creative autonomy" in to a realization of the vedantic unity of all life. The separate individuals come to progressively perceive the "good of all" through undertaking a life of loving service. The vision of the common "good of all" is impeded in so far as one is taught, or acquires the bad bhavana of "I am the body". This attitude is not however confined to merely one's physical body but was extended to include any attachment whatsoever. Vinoba explains "attachment to family" is "attachment to nation". That is, attachment to one's particular family in this context, erects a spiritual barrier to realizing the human family while attachment to nation similarly impedes the essential idea that we are all citizens of the world. Truly, every object including "government" had two forms : an outer body (which breeds attachment) and an inner soul (worthy of devotion). Vinoba observed that "Sarvodaya" stands for "freedom from government, it means decentralization of power." becomes significant. He further distinguished the "freedom from government" objective from "no government" ideal in so far as in the former "government" functions are modeled "upon the divine government – unseen, unfelt and decentralized. Thus in so far as "government" is decentralized it represents the divine ideal – the ideal of Ram Rajya, the Kingdom of God, becoming into concrete existence. Vinoba terms "anarchism" might be better described as "anti-statism" or a dislike of all government to the extent to which it is centralized. The "State" or the "body aspect" of "government" which is reflected in the principle of centralization is present in all existing government. While referring to those in the Sarvodaya Movement, Vinoba noted that:

> "We do not believe in the very institution of Centralized Government...... this is a fundamental point of principle. And on this point, my position is there with all governments in the world, not excluding my own."

Vinoba says, as the bhavana of "I am the body" implies the achieving of the "I am the Self" attitude, so also does the bhavana of "statism" prevent the individual from realizing that Swaraj or self-government means "ruling your own self". The State may not provide its citizens with valuable material benefits since political power can be an instrument of service. However, "the good work which is done by government services is very far from good in its effect upon the minds of the people" he admitted. Another danger consistent is that the State might actually provide all of the services necessary for its citizens. It is really conceivable to provide ample opportunity for physical work if it is considered a "need" of the citizen. Vinoba would seem to have considered such a policy as unlikely especially since an attitude of general laziness would have been prompted in other areas. If however a programme of mandatory labour was to be enforced by the State, either physically or through subtle indoctrination, Vinoba would still have opposed to it. This opposition would be best understood by a thorough examination of Vinoba's statement that :

> "It is one mark of swaraj not to allow any outside power in the world to exercise control over oneself. And the second mark of swaraj is not to exercise power over any other.....no submission and no exploitation."

To allow oneself to be ruled by external forces meant that one is not "ruling oneself" which is the essence of individual swaraj. To have attained to this swaraj is more over to have voluntarily surrendered oneself to the rule of "niti" the moral law, which consists of one's performing one's swadharma. By presumption the individual as a karma yogin must seek self realization on his or her own for the State (or even tradition) to enforce a particular dharma upon one must be resisted. "Where there is a raj, a coercive government, niti is destroyed" because limitations are thereby placed upon the internal rule of the "moral law". On the other hand, to exercise power over others in the sense of exploiting them for one's own ends, destroys individuals swaraj as the ego is given new life by such activity. According to Vinoba, this would not only increase the rajasic element in one's nature but would in addition violate the categorical imperative by not doing "unto others as you would have them do unto you". In both cases the realization of the spiritual end would be impeded by the law of karma which decrees that what is sown shall be reaped. Thus according to Vinoba "One is a real lover of freedom who feels that one also must not rule over others."

To the extent to which individual swaraj is both allowed and fought for that the ideal of Ramrajya is approached. Within Vinoba's religious conceptual framework, this means "the standard of life should be distinguished from the standard of living". While the "Welfare State" may serve to increase the standard of living, it fails to increase the "standard of life" which is not so dependent upon material satisfactions. Therefore, the Welfare State is an ill-fated State by impeding the spiritual development of people. Therefore, to the extent, the power comes to be concentrated in the hands of the State even a Welfare State acting in the service of its citizens, the rule of niti is reduced and spiritual barriers are placed along the path of individual swaraj. Since all centralization of power in government was thus quite logically considered to be to the spiritual detriment of individuals how much greater is the detriment, when the State can make the masses believe it "represents" them, according to Vinoba. Thus the conclusion is implicit that representative democracy stifles the development of each person as a spiritual being. He argued :

> "The truth is that no real freedom exists today, and we shall not get it so long as we carry on with

> our "representative democracy" and do not take the management of our village affairs into our own hands."

The State may be identified with "government" "representative democracy" correspondingly connotes a condemnable form of "democracy". In that form, Vinoba complained about how the mass of citizens take it "as a matter of course that anything to be done is the responsibility of the elected representatives." They become "sheep" who allowing the State to perform much of their svadharma for them, become spiritually impoverished even as they may be materially benefited. He would, in this context agree that:

> "The fundamental problem is the powerlessness and fatalism of the people..... their lack of faith in themselves and the future they are capable of building."

The Swatantra Loka Shakti or "self reliant power of the people" can only be generated as a new bhavana is adopted which maintains that a participatory democracy "the people are everything and the government nothing". The attitude that "the State has power over me" must be abandoned as power passes "in to the hands of the people" in more than rhetorical sense. He claimed that representative democracy is "only a formal democracy" because people really only exercise power at election time, thus leaving the representative-elite free to rule, in interim periods, as they please. For the masses to experience a liberation from their sheepish attitudes, Vinoba concluded, they must actively participate as karma yogins in both the formulation and execution of policies. It is in this context Vinoba observed how the "essence of democracy lies in the control of people over the government" To the extent that people as individuals "control" the government, that "government" becomes decentralized and the power of the State is reduced. This process of decentralization, which was viewed as approaching the ideal of Ram Rajya, involves a progressive emphasis upon small scale units, like villages, as the main units of government. Larger units, like regional federations, would be countenanced as helpful for purposes of coordination of non-violent defense and utilization of resources, but would also be without recognised power to enforce their decisions. Thus the mass of people would be given free reign to participate in all matters which affect their lives and spiritual growth would be enhanced in the process.

Vinoba's allegiance to the primary of small village units confines his notion of a justifiable polity to an extremely decentralized level. The concept of "nation", for example is rendered as unnecessary as the perceived necessity for delegating authority in a large, centralized unit. Vinoba was infact repudiating the developmental course of many areas which define "progress" mainly in material terms. In his village society ideal the spiritual "progress" of people of moksha (true freedom) was of the foremost importance and decentralized as the structure may be, delegation of authority through such means as election was considered quite unnecessary.

Vinoba, further opposed the "election demon" because the formal right to vote was, in his view, "like the right of the sheep to elect a shepherd." Instead of encouraging the masses to individual performance of svadharma, it promotes a bhavana of having done one's duty at the ballot box. As it discourages, continued participation in the political process it increases the centralization of power in the hands of a few. Indeed it is not difficult to perceive how Vinoba concluded that.

> "The whole arrangement, in fact, is sheer bogus....It does even more harm than our former kings could do because our governments can now claim to "represent public opinion."

Vinoba had a fundamental dislike for the principle of majority rule in addition to objecting to the veil of legitimacy constructed by virtue of elections. He recognised that majority rule reflects the doctrine of "the greatest good for the greatest number" – a dictum which inherently denies the Sarvodaya view of "the common good of all." It promotes a bhavana in which individual conflicts of interest are treated as real and fundamental – quite contrary to the Sarvodaya teaching. The majority rule principle also violates the means-ends relationship. Vinoba asked:

> "Is not the rule of majority only brute force ? How can you differentiate between the rule of the regiment, rule of money and rule of the majority?"

Vinoba further asserted, "right and wrong cannot be decided by majority vote." In his conception only the individuals should decide what is right and wrong – although there is a place for opinion leaders who, by virtue of the respect they hold within a community, exercise greater influence in decision making. Vinoba argued, only when utilizing the principle of consensus, this "greater influence" be reconciled with the duty of all to participate. Responsibility for deciding "right or wrong" is thus never really delegated in his consensus alternative. Whether or not consensus democracy is a desirable or practical alternative to rule by majority is too complex a matter to do justice to here. Consensus does not require unanimous agreement. A decision is deferred until there is no active opposition to it being implemented. In other words any majority must take into account the majority perspective if any decision is to be arrived at. From a practical standpoint all would be more likely to seek out the "common good of all" since it would be in their perceived "self-interest" to do so. A spirit of co-operation, in consonance with the Sarvodaya ideal would, moreover, be much more emphasized than in any alternative scheme. As per Vinoba "Election and other works decided upon by the majority of opinion, in the name of democracy, have spread the poison of rivalry between parties and organisations in villages". According to him, "caste-differences have been fostered by elections in the country." It is entirely fictitious to believe that party politics leads to the welfare of the people because among other reasons, parties indulge in bargain driving by their nature, while "the only kind of 'service' worthy of the name is disinterested service." Disservice is done as rivalries are promoted thus enhancing the bhavana of "I am the body". In the Sarvodaya view : "We will have to rise up above the petty considerations of caste, creed, language or province" but political parties emphasize such distinctions for their own political advantage. Vinoba says:

> "If any spirit of bargaining, any tendency to invoke legal sanctions, enters into the mutual relationships of two citizens, it destroys the mutual relationships of two citizens, it destroys the mutual trust and sense of fellowship between them."

> "Bargaining" is further condemned even though Vinoba admitted that differences in view are "necessary and inevitable". Each individual's duty or dharma, is to do what he or she believes to be right according to the perception of truth at any given point in time. Bargaining in this context is a violation of dharma, while a free exchange of relative perceptions of truth contributes to the individual's growth into a new dharma or higher consciousness of truth. So, in his point, parties

> stand condemned on the ground that loyalty to a party often overrides loyalty to the pursuit of truth that is God. Genuine criticism is stifled as the people become sheep to a shepherd's party and honest criticism from opposition parties is frequently dismissed as partisan. In this opinion framework, he concluded that "to participate in the party system and in elections is to increase the stranglehold of party politics. Vinoba however opposed political parties also; By casting our vote in favour of some party, we subordinate ourselves to power, we hardly do anything ourselves. A bad bhavana, in other words is fostered in which individuals tend to surrender their svadharma to others. His individual karma yoga base thus promoted him to remind us that "Lord Krishna enjoins upon as in the Gita that our deliverance has to be achieved by us only."

Sarvodaya is not a "party" and is "non partisan" in its approach. It is a theory which advises its adherents to "take part in political activities but not in political groupings" since they "must live like lions, not turn into sheep." His opinion that power tends to corrupt. Vinoba while admitted that there are some great souls who can keep their detachment even while holding a place of authority. In general the temptations of office are such as to corrupt most people. According to Vinoba, the tendency is for the office holder or the party leader to "become narrow in outlook" as one becomes enamored of the power position. This fosters the rajasic element in one's nature and, hence, one's ego thereby serving to impede the destruction of the same. Vinoba says:

> "The problem lies at the very nature of authority.....(since) in general, the field of sacrifice. It does not afford natural opportunities for renunciation.

The function of developing "the power of the people" was not in this context capturing the political power so much as dispersing it. Such decentralization of government allows for more citizen participation and, thereby the development of "the strength of the people". As the karma yogin undertakes action in a bhavana of bhakti (Dedicating all fruits to God = Society), individual spiritual strength or swaraj is achieved. He observed that:

> "The politics of power is one thing while that of strength is another. People generally go after "power politics" but power cramps strength which increases with detached service".

Vinoba further says that "never accept political power". He significantly agreed with Marx that the State in any centralized administrative or coercive sense, will "wither away". This meant "there will be no State authority towards the end" and "the governance of the country will go on without the interference or function of any central power". Ram Rajya is no certainty. Thus in Vinoba's view :

> "It is only when large group of people....aloof from positions or political power, but......endowed with the power of discretion and devoted in every way to service, sacrifice and study is formed on a permanent basis that the task of purifying....would be accomplished."

Vinoba on the other hand maintained that until the "peoples' power" (or "strength of the people") is sufficiently developed, the society needs a State and the State ought not to be directly attacked. The right form of government depends upon the stage of development reached by people. Such a position is not to say that the best form is not signified in the ideal of Ram Rajya. Vinoba realized :

> "We have got to remember that although our present political system may not be a genuine government by the people, it is certainly government by the consent of the people. To change it we must change the people...."

Vinoba never explicitly defined what is meant by "good government" as an intermediate stage between centralized government and freedom from government, he mentioned that in it the masses given their consent to be ruled by "capable individuals." On the one hand, Vinoba implied that the "capable individuals" are the Sarvodaya movement's karma yogins who agree that "the politics of today....will change only when the people change." These workers would be "capable" by virtue of their own spiritual attainments and would, consistently, have authority only in proportion as the masses love them for their services. They would endeavor, through their actions, to teach by example the message they would have the masses embrace. In his message of Sarvodaya he proclaims that:

> "I live in the village and that village is an integral part of the world. God is our ruler and we, of the village, run our village-state by mutual consent and cooperative effort. They would identify themselves neither with the government nor with the people. They should be independent of both, and render true service to both, by pointing out the virtues and faults of both sides, being friends of all but members of no party."

Vinoba on the other hand, held that "to disclaim the authorship of all action is superior to capability" thus strongly implying that his "capable individuals" are not the karma yogins of the movement. Instead of standing "in between the rulers and the ruled" they would seem to stand as the rulers of the State whose objective may be "to see that every villager is his own ruler." Today, in this context, a "capable individual" becomes capable only "by mutual assistance" and has "authority only to serve the people" would appear to be but a feeble camouflage for an elitist rationale for change. Such an impression is reinforced by his observation that even if Government takes the form of "rule by one", still "if it is based on non-violence it should in reality be regarded as "rule by all". As there are only individuals who are more or less capable, the burden of raising the consciousness of the masses falls heavily upon those who are "capable" in any "good government" stage of development. Vinoba observed that:

> "Those without education, without money, without land...cannot be expected to think about democracy. Hence this responsibility falls on.....those who own land and wealth."

Vinoba particularly in Swaraj Sastra revealed that by "capable individuals" he meant, not the karma yogins who have renounced wealth and land, but the physically strong, the wealthy and the privileged. Such people, attached to their possessions and hardly expected to proceed forth in a bhavana of bhakti, would seem incapable of teaching swaraj to others. Indeed, within Vinoba's framework they cannot even approach swaraj for themselves! Vinoba believed "if the principle of representation must, be denounced as a means incapable of attaining to the ideal of Ram Rajya so also must a theory of "capable individuals" be dismissed. The law of karma tells that "we reap what we sow" centralization leads to centralization and capable individuals give rise to others attached to the bhavana of "I am the body" To depend upon "capable" individuals would be little different from dependence upon "capable" representatives. Other individuals not so detached would almost invariably be corrupted by power. Such people would in the least predictably seek to have State Policy force the masses to be free. Vinoba however observed that "in a good State non-cooperation and resistance are occasional and depend on time and place." Vinoba consistently opposed to any "dictatorship of the proletariat" conception during the intermediate, "good government" stage. He observed, accordingly that "decentralization of the power of the state should begin even now" arguing that "If the goodness in man is not relied upon the State will never wither away at any time."

At this point it would be well to remember that the power of the State is exhibited in "the coercive power of law" (*danda shakti*). Law is thus divisive and since, like the State's actions generally, it promotes a bhavana of separation and of being ruled, Vinoba expressed concluded that "Legislation should not be forced on people." It would appear, to be as logically an impure means of producing lok niti as centralization of power is for an end of decentralization. Again there arises an inconsistency with regard to danda shakti to parallel that of his "capable individuals" doctrine. While on the one hand he proclaimed that "we must realize that to accept government aid will weaken our vigor, understanding and strength" on other other hand he as so "anxious to provide a base to constructive work" as to allow it to "be supplied either by official legislation or by public approval." He further states that:

> "Legislation may be of violent or non-violent nature and it may tilt towards either. If a legislative measure, even if it has the backing of the electorate, is not of a non-violent nature, that legislation itself will be violence."

We fail to understand how any legislation unless adopted by unanimous consent or unless devoid of punitive provisions, could qualify as being of a "non-violent" nature given Vinoba's framework. Such legislation, whether accomplished by a minority or a majority of the population would in either case be as much an example of "brute force" to those opposed as majority rule was argued by Vinoba to be for a minority. Moreover that legislation is "non-violent" if it reflects or is supported by "the power of the people". Vinoba however qualified his sanction of the use of law by observing that:

> "If a particular reform is voluntarily adopted by a number of individuals and if that voluntary action prepares the public mind for the change, then whatever little work is left to be done could be achieved through the process of law."

Vinoba believed that "the place for legislation.....comes last." this would seem to obviate any severe departure from principle as might occur if legislation were utilized as a primary means of bringing about change. The uses of the law are not for the morally good or for the morally bad, but for the morally weak. These "morally weak" persons are conscious that physical violence is undesirable and have thus evolved beyond the mentality of the "morally bad". Still they have not attained consciousness of "moral goodness" which in the freedom from government stage of Ram Rajya, renounces all coercion. Briefly, the "morally work" are those who in the intermediate stage of "good government" need the State and insist upon using laws because they are "ignorant of the power of the soul". He realized that the kinds of service done for the people by the State through laws are "not the kind of service which may be conducive to creating the conditions which will do away with the use of law. Legislations and the actions of "capable individuals" might lay a material foundation which, satisfying the needs of the body, may help the *bhavana* of "I am the body" to be overcome. True spiritual salvation, could only be attained to by individual *karma yogins* seeking swaraj by performance of *svadharma* in a *bhavana* of *bhakti*. While it is therefore "the character of the people and not the particular system in which they are bound together that guarantees justice" that "character" is nevertheless, a function of how decentralized the power of the State has become. The greater the participation of the masses and through participation, the more their swaraj grows. True democracy in small units and without representatives, parties or voting, becomes in this context not merely a means, but also an end : "the end being the self development of individuals."

Vinoba therefore concluded by observing how "cracy" is strong while "demos" is weak. Cracy represented by institutions of representation (centralization) and such utilitarian instruments as elections and majority rule have become impediments in the fight to overcome the *bhavana* that "I am the body". Indeed according to Vinoba, representative democracy" is committing suicide everywhere and the only remedy is to bring *lok niti* into being." The suicide, while spiritual in the sense that the people have become slaves (in their attitude) to the representatives, is also political in the sense that an elite can, in the egoistic interest engendered by virtue of their power, exploit others for their own ends. Representative democracy, is, in this, analysis, held to be contrary to the development of each person as a spiritual being. That Vinoba muddied the clarity of this position by inconsistently alluding to doctrines of "capable individuals" and of "non-violent laws" in the intermediate stages of "God government" does not detract from his main line of reasoning. *Swatantra loka shakti* develops as individuals acting and interacting in society come to realize progressively greater self-rule (*swaraj*). As the rule of *niti* (the moral law) evolves into existence through the efforts of *karma yogins* performing *svadharma* in a *bhavana* of *bhakti*, the ideal of Ram Rajya was thought to become more and more concrete in its being.

References

- Vinoba, Speeches cited by D.D. Moondara, Sant Vinoba ki Uttar Bharat Yatra.
- H. Tennyson, Saint on the March.
- Jayaprakash Narayan, Socialism, Sarvodaya and Democracy.
- S. Ram, Vinoba and His Mission.
- Vinoba's Speech inside the Jail. As cited by S.K. Bhatta, Chambal Ke Beharon Men.

8

The Dream of Gram Swaraj

Vinoba came to a conclusion towards a next step to provide a better life and better living condition for the people. Bhoodan and Gramdan are merely a means to achieve the end – "Gram Swaraj" or "Village – Self Government". His main thesis behind this concept was to bring about a change in the economic and political set-up of the country and establish a new social order through peaceful means. The concentration of power at the Centre or the State level would not make the people of the villages feel the true spirit of Swaraj until the powers are delegated to them and village autonomy is recognized in principle as well as implemented in actual practice. The economic powers in India should be decentralized as far as possible and the villages through a process of planning from below should be made strong and self-reliant. This freedom "Gram Swaraj" would certainly ensure a better life and living to every individual. Even though the literal meaning of Gram Swaraj is village-self rule, it has a deeper and wider connotation. It indicates democratic decentralization and carries with it a solid economic programme as well. In fact, freedom remains lopsided if there is economic dis-equalibrium in a country. Political independence cannot be maintained without economic equality. Gram Swaraj therefore should aim at the politico-economic decentralization. On the one hand it sanctions the political freedom to the people of the villages and on the other hand the economic power to plan their growth and development. The term "Swaraj" is a compound sanskrit word derived from "Swa" and "Rajya" which signify "rule over self". Swaraj thus means self-disciplined exercise by individuals to attain their economic and political ends. Gram Swaraj thus recognises individual and social action for improving the economic life of the people.

The Indian village communities have been in existence since the earlier times. The villages have remained the unchanging backbone of Indian life. In Chhandogya Upanishad there was a reference of an ideal State. In the kingdom of King Ashwapati there was no thief, no miser, no drunkard, no ignorant, no unchaste man and woman. The existence of "Gram Sanghas" or village federations in the Vedic Age were evident. In the Shantiparva of Mahabharata it has been told that the village self-governments were controlling the social, political and economic life in order to promote human dignity and social justice. These were found a sound system of production, distribution and taxation. Kautilya in his Arthashastra has described the nature and scope of State activities. The King was regarded as the trustee of the villages and was to regulate all types of economic and social activities. Agriculture and Industries were the main occupations. Lord Elphinstone once said : The village communities contain in miniature all the materials of a State within themselves and are almost sufficient to protect their members, if all other governments are withdrawn." Sir Charles T. Metcalfe, the Acting Governor General had recorded :

> "The Union of the village communities, each one forming a separate little State in itself, has, I conceive, contributed more than any other cause to the preservation of the people of India through all revolutions and changes which they have suffered and it is in a high degree conducive to their happiness and to the enjoyment of a great portion of freedom and independence. I wish, therefore, that the village constitutions may never be disturbed and I dread everything that has a tendency to break them up."

Even though India took different shapes from the Rig Vedic Kingdom to Guptas Monarchy and later the empires of the Mughals and Britishers, yet the village community persisted and effectively developed on its own lines. The communities had exhibited two forms : one the territorial and the other the functional.

Through "Gram Swaraj" which was often called "Ram Raj", Gandhiji's aim was to revive the old village culture. His strong belief that the non-violent economy can only flourish in small units has held him to act for village republics instead of pleading for the Metropolis culture of highly industrialised order which thrives on exploitation and violence. He firmly believed that without truth and non-violence, the destruction of humanity is inevitable. If India is to attain freedom sooner or later the fact must be recognised that people will have to live in villages, not in towns, in huts, not in palaces. Living in town, they will never be able to have peace. The highly industrialised States, whether capitalist or communist, always try to extend their economic domain. Instead of colonialism, they create economic imperialism and dependencies. Gandhiji explained "My dream of village Swaraj is that it is a complete republic, independent of its neighbours for its own vital wants and yet interdependent for may others in which dependence is a necessity. Thus every village's first concern will be to grow its own food crops and cotton for its cloth." Gram Swaraj, according to him, is the foundation of true democracy in India. They are mostly self-centered, party-dominated and power-oriented. Gandhiji thus observed "true democracy cannot be worked by twenty men sitting at the Centre."

Vinoba's Swaraj Sastra is the extension of Gandhian philosophy of non-violence in the realm of political and economic theory. He has minutely observed the principles of State regulation to conceive clearly the idea underlying "Swaraj". Vinoba undertook the task of interpreting the fundamental principles which govern a non-violent political and social order. Vinoba makes a clear distinction between "Rajya" and "Swaraj" that is distinction between Government and Self-Government. A Government can be had through violence. Self Government is impossible without non-violence. According to him, the Government is best which governs the least. It is not static organisation that runs on some rigid methodology but one that changes its path according to the levels of development desired in a society. The social and cultural changes, the changes in the levels of technology, and the structural and institutional changes alter the principles of State regulation and consequently upon them the forms of government also undergo a change. Despite of all these changes, there are some fundamental principles which are universal and govern the State in establishing the permanent values of human life. As per Vinoba, Swaraj means the total transformation of human life and the establishment of new values of truth, non-violence and compassion. A society of such an order cannot be created by the politics of power

(Rajniti) but by the politics of the people (Lokniti). Thus both are different from each other. The power politics aims at the cenralization of State authority and curtailment of individual liberty. But the politics of people on the other hand recognises the freedom of action, devolves the power and creates the spirit of service and co-operation in the society.

Only Lokniti can establish true democratic values in society. The basis of this is "Jan Shakti" i.e. the power of the people as opposed to "Dand Shakti" i.e. the legal power of the State. Jan Shakti plays a vital role in the organisation of society and in its administration. But the people must be given real power and not fake. Sri Jayaprakash Narayan while criticising the western democracy rightly remarked : "The whole process of democracy rests on the arithmetic of votes. The individual voter casts his vote as an atom of society, not as a living cell in the organic relationship with other living cells. Vinoba at this juncture introduced his own theory of true democratic values. Modern civilization needs social integration. Man should not be regarded as an isolated individual but integral part of the social framework. Self-governing communities built upon personal relationship, freedom of action and a common culture should be regarded as the basis of the modern social order. The purpose of a "more adequate democracy" is to bring the people to a common platform and teach them to participate in government - "a participating democracy". Therefore, true democratic values are the familiarisation of society, common man's participation in the government, the freedom of choice and action, the creation of Jan-Shakti and above all "the right to commit mistake" as defined by Gandhiji in Gram Swaraj.

Vinoba's Gram Swaraj is not confined to the political set up alone. It is a triple programme of purification, reconstruction and development. It is a Trinity of Gramdan, village industries and Shanti Sena. Gramdan movement forms the main basis of Gram Swaraj. It is an organisation of the people where they voluntarily unite and discard the ownership of land. They create a certain harmony among themselves and a distinct consciousness which encourages a feeling of collective and of community spirit. Vinoba claims Gramdan alone will not suffice unless it is accompanied by Village Industries and Shanti Sena. Hence Vinoba chalked out a three-fold programme embracing all the important aspects of village life. Village Industries are the back bone of rural economy. Hence he made this an integral part of the Gramdan Movement. Shanti Sena is the third programme which is composed of a band of selfless workers who strive for maintaining peace and serve the society with their steadfast devotion. A shanti Sainik is a devoted servant of the people who looks after the village affairs in a selfless way. Thus, the trinity of Gramdan, Village Industries and Peace Brigade form the basis of India's rural reconstruction through a non-violent process. Gramdan generates common will. Khadi gives the economic resource and Shanti Sena enlarges the sphere of peace and non-violence. Hence Vinoba has outlined this triple programme for the village so that the country may usher in a new period of prosperity of Gram Swaraj.

The Government at a stage realised the importance of democratic decentralization. The Balwantrai Mehta Committee in 1957 had strongly recommended for an easy and direct process of people's participations in the framework of local units to accelerate the development programmes of the country. It had also realised that too much power had been centralized in a few hands and very little active co-operation was offered by the people in making the national planning a success. For devolving power, Panchayati Raj was introduced in India. Panchayat Raj stands for the right of self determination and for forming the village governments. It is an attempt to decentralize democratic institutions. Article 40 of our Constitution lays down that the State shall take steps to organize village Panchayats and endow them with such powers and authority as may be necessary to enable them to function as units of self-government. Panchayats are the representative units of government and not merely bodies to execute the development programmes. Even though Panchayati Raj closes the door for "participating democracy" at the higher levels.

Panchayati Raj as an integrated social organisation can only be established through Gramdan. Since the elections are fought on party basis, and also the mass poverty and illiteracy, higher and lower caste concepts, owner and worker mentality have led the villages to the most unhappy consequences. Hence it is in this respect, Gramdan is the only suitable instrument for establishing Panchayati Raj. Gramdan creates a right climate for Panchayat organisations. It makes all the people equal. When the right of ownership is discarded by the people themselves, their grouping together for a common cause becomes easier and most effective. There are no distinctions between the high and the low or between the poor and the rich. The spirit of power dominates the Panchayat rather than the spirit of service. The majority forms the deciding factor instead of unanimity or decision by Consensus. Therefore the real Panchayati Raj is possible only through Gramdans. The success of the Panchayati Raj depends upon economic and structural changes which are brought about by the Gramdan movement. No amount of activities and progress of Panchayati Raj can bring about as vital a change in the society as the Gramdan movement is capable of because it goes deep into the hearts of the people to find out the hidden treasure of love and sympathy, of follow-feeling and co-operation.

Gram Swaraj is impossible unless the economic base is strengthened by decentralization. Decentralization is a process through which means of production and distribution are not centrally controlled but are maintained by small democratic units to regulate the economy in the interest of the society as a whole and not of any group or individual. It does not mean dispersal of industries. Such an economy is essentially a non-violent and non-exploiting one. It aims at just and equitable distribution of private and social gains. Dispersion implies "scattered ness" that may take various forms. A centralized order stands on a weak foundation with a heavy top involves a good risk. Hence there is a need for a balanced economic development in the society. It should aim at the wholesome progress of each and every individual and tries to integrate the social and economic life of the people. Thus a balanced economy means to return to nature what is taken away from it. Therefore in this context, the idea of village self-sufficiency comes into the picture. Villages must be made self-sufficient in order to have a sound and integrated economic growth. Such a village would be independent economic units, relying on their own resources for basic needs. A self-sufficient village economy is strong enough to fight even against the forces of monetary and fiscal disruptions as it chiefly utilizes local resources and can possibly maintain itself for a longer period during the crisis. If we are to maintain Nature's equilibrium then the whole consumer's goods should be locally produced and consumed, which can be achieved through regional planning. The self-sufficient economy has a network of concentric circles of productive resources and requirements. Thus the lesser the degree of a requirement, the bigger will be the circles of self-sufficiency. In order to achieve a balanced economy and self-sufficiency the complete set up of planning has to be re-oriented. Since the majority of the people living in villages, planning must start from there. A centralized planning proves to be ineffective and inefficient in this case. Acharya Vinoba Bhave who originated the idea of Gramdan, has paved the way for village planning on the lines of Sarvodaya philosophy.

Life has become stale and flat in both, the cities and the villages. The growing population have created many problems. The rural-urban equation has become unbalanced and meaningless. Sri Jayaprakash Narayan has suggested that for a proper balance agriculture and industry must be carried on together in an interdependent and complementary manner. In our country the rural-urban population rations are so disproportionate that the rural sector finds it difficult to cope with the demands of the urban sector. Hence he demands complete abolition of the rural-urban concept. Technology is also playing an important role. The adoption of a higher level of technology by an underdeveloped country is neither economically beneficial nor socially desirable. It creates unemployment by displacing the worker from the job and also costs more as regards the capital investment "per-work-place." Moreover the low cost products of the high level technology cannot be so advantageous as the higher cost products of a lower level of technology. It was for this reason that Mahatma pleaded for Khadi which though costly as compared to the mill cloth, was socially profitable. Because of the above reasons, the Indian economy should not go for heavy industrialization. Because our country is an agricultural one and will continue to be one for decades, secondly the economy has a large untapped human potential in the abundant labour supply. Therefore the industries should be based on the indigenous resources of labour and capital and a level of technology should be so evolved as to provide for greater employment opportunities to the people with the minimum investment. The industrialization must not be centralized and villages should be given ample opportunity to industrialize themselves in the manner they need and desire.

Vinoba has called upon members of the All India Congress Committee in its session at Behrampur on May 9, 1955 to devote the next two years to the Bhoodan movement. In an hour long address, he said that the movement, based on non-violence, had certain spiritual implications and working for it would actually amount to strengthening world peace. This is the first time that he has addressed the AICC. For the first time in history fear complex was pervading the world and this could be put an end to only when a spirit of fearlessness was infused. Fearlessness could not be achieved through the possession of weapons. The cultivation of Ahimsa alone could give man fearlessness.

References

- The Draft Manifesto of the Sarvodaya Movement (Nagpur: Sarva Seva Sangh, 1973).
- Indu Tikekar, Integral Revolution : An Analytical Study of Gandhian Though (Varanasi : Sarva Seva Sangh Prakashan, 1970).
- Vinoba Bhave, Talks on Gita (Varanasi : Sarva Seva Sangh Prakashan, 1970).
- Vinoba Bhave, Swaraj Sastra (Kashi : Sarva Seva Sangh Prakashan, 1959).
- Vinoba Bhave, Gramdan for Gramswaraj (Varanasi : Sarva Seva Sangh Prakashan, 1967).
- Vinoba Bhave, Democratic Values and the Practice of Citizenship (Kashi : Sarva Seva Sangh Prakashan, [illegible]).

- Vinoba Bhave, Revolutionary Sarvodaya (Bombay, Bharatiya Vidya Bhavan, 1964).
- Vinoba, Gramdan for Gramswaraj.
- Vinoba, Elections and Democracy.
- Vishwanath Tandon, the Social and Political Philosophy of Sarvodaya after Gandhi (Varanasi : Sarva Seva Sangh Prakashan).
- Dada Dharmadhikari, Introduction to Democratic Values.
- Ostergaad and Currel, The Gentle Anarchists.

9

Implications of Gram Swaraj

The Gramdan villages donated to Vinoba have their own planning for development. They try to become self-reliant and self-sufficient as far as the basic necessities of life specifically food and clothing are concerned. They concentrate mostly on cottage industries and convert local raw materials into finished products. Having faith in non-violence, they settle their disputes amicably and try to live like a family.

Diwan Shatrughan Singh, one of the richest landlords of the village Mangroth in Hamirpur district of Uttar Pradesh and a devoted social worker has had in his mind a revolutionary idea of bringing about a change in the social and economic set up of the village since his early years of his life. He had actively participated in the freedom struggle of the country and had commanded great respect among the local people of the village as a true patriot and their able guide as well. In 1952, Diwan Shatrughan Singh attended the Sarvodaya Conference at Sevapuri, Varanasi. He met Vinoba and was highly impressed by the ideology and the working of the Bhoodan mission. Later he invited Vinoba to come to his home at village Mangroth. Vinoba too accepted his invitation.

On his return to Mangroth, Diwan Shatrughan Singh consulted the village people about donating the whole land of the village to Vinoba. He met the landholders individually, explained his idea and the pattern of life which he wanted to bring to the village through Vinoba's Gramdan Movement. On 23rd May, 1952, Vinoba crossed the river Betwa and came to Mangroth. However he had not stayed there long since the programmes were already fixed. The day Vinoba left Mangroth "without any dan" made the people restless. Since the concept was not clear, the people of the village called on Diwan and asked him to explain its meaning and interpretation. Diwan Shatrughan Singh then told the people that the land would remain with them; only the ownership would have to be discarded. It was like sharing one's food with God. The people of the village except one land owner convinced and decided to donate the land to Vinoba. On 24th May, 1952, Diwan Shatrughan Singh went to Rath where Vinoba was staying, prostrated himself at the feet of Vinoba and surrendered the whole village adding humbly that it was only a small gift from the people of Mangroth. It came as a surprise to Vinoba. Infact he could not believe it. The first Bhoodan he had received a year back and now he got an entire village in donation. Vinoba questioned himself 'Was not this the Will of God?' The two points made a line and the path was clear before him. From Bhoodan to Gramdan was thus the natural step.

Vinoba deputed Shri Karan Bhai for giving advice to the villagers as after the donation of the village some important decisions were taken concerning the use of land and its management. He went to Mangroth in April, 1953 as an expert in village activities and constructive programmes, studied the local conditions. The main problem before him was to decide the future pattern of cultivation to be adopted by the people. Discussions were held among the villagers relating to the adoption of collective, co-operative or individual farming and came to the following conclusions:-

(i) All land belongs to the village as a whole but cultivation to the farmers;

(ii) Agriculture and employment should be adopted on family basis;

(iii) Farmers are free to adopt either of the two types of farmings: Collective or Individual

(iv) The Gram Sabha should renew the individual occupancy right every year;

(v) The land revenue shall not be paid to the Government separately but collectively through the Sarvodaya Mandal.

The villagers pledged to work with full co-operation and sincerity. They adopted individual cultivation as well as collective. The cultivation is commonly performed through animal driven ploughs as the land is uneven and terrain makes mechanical farming difficult. The cultivators use chemical fertilizers for crop production. There had been remarkable progress in the sphere of agricultural production. Before the Gramdan, there was scarcity of food grains as the village could meet requirement of ten to eleven months. However after the Gramdan the production had gone up considerably and reached its peak in 1960-61 due to the collective efforts to construct a minor canal, erection of Bandhs, conserving the soil and adopting proper methods and techniques of cultivation.

After the Gramdan, in Mangroth, the industries of spinning, weaving and leather works were started. Apart from these, the people of the village were engaged in cottage industries such as oil milling, carpet and rope making, pottery works, wood works, fishing, and dairy farming. In Mangroth an Ashram had been established which is mainly responsible for the industrial production and constructive activities of the village. Leather and Shoe-making industry is the biggest and most popular industry of the village. Thirteen families are engaged in leather dyeing and six families prepare shoes. Apart from this, a full fledged shoe-production department had been opened in June 1967 with the aid of Gandhi-Smarak-Nidhi. The raw material for dyeing the leather is available from the leaves of 'Dhau' tree from the jungles of the village. The skin of the died animals are used. The traditional shoes of Mangroth are very famous. They are long sized and are turned upwards at the toe. They have got a very good market at Rath and Orai. Spinning and Weaving Industry is the second biggest industry of the village. About thirty men and women were fully engaged in the weaving work. Before Gramdan this industry was decaying fast due to non-availability of raw materials. But after Gramdan a Khadi Center for the training of the village people was opened under the Khadi development scheme of the Uttar Pradesh Government. This has resulted in making almost a spinner in every family. The Sarvodaya Mandal is bestowing much care on this industry. Ambar Charkha Training Center was also opened and the Mandal is trying to organise the industry on collective lines. Next, Oil Milling is a very old industry of the village. The oil-seeds produced in the village are crushed in the 'wooden rahtas' to take out oil. four families were engaged in this work. Sarvodaya Mandal has arranged for a co-operative scheme of oil milling in the village. It has established a "Ghani" to increase the production of oil. The village is now not only sufficient in oil but exports its mustard oil to the neighbouring suburban markets. Fishing is also one of the several activities of the village people. About twenty five persons work as fishermen and fishing from the river Betwa on contract basis. Apart from these, there are several activities like dairy farming, pottery and wood works.

After the declaration of Gramdan, the administrative body of Mangroth was constituted. On June 15, 1953 Vinoba sent an authority letter transferring the right of ownership of land and management to the Sarvodaya Mandal. Mangroth was registered in the name of Sarvodaya Mandal under the Societies Registration Act, 1860. The following are the main features of the constitution:

(a) *Aims and Objectives*. The main objectives of this Mandal is to establish the village self government in Mangroth by means of Gramdan, which will be based on equality and self-dependence. The social organisation brought about by this Mandal shall ensure that there would be no exploitation of any short and every man and woman, leading the life of a real worker, shall be provided with full opportunity to develop his or her individuality and economic life. To fulfill the above objective the Mandal will organise land and agriculture of the village; will collect and spend wealth on behalf of its members; will possess and own movable and immovable property and preserve the right of its sale and transfer etc.

(b) *Membership.* Every villager after twenty years of age shall be the member of the Sarvodaya Mandal. The outsider can also become a member if he wishes to settle down at the village and satisfies the Mandal with his conduct. The new bride from the day she comes to the village shall automatically be the member of the Mandal.

(c) *Working Committee.* The working committee will consist of fifteen members. Five members shall retire annually by rotation and shall be replaced by election. The president will be selected unanimously. The working committee will select a secretary and joint secretary every year.

(d) *Trustee Mandal.* It is a decorative unit of the Sarvodaya Mandal. It will consist of nine members – four life long members and five selected by working committee. The Trustee Mandal would see that Sarvodaya Mandal is carrying on its work properly.

(e) *Powers and Duties of the Working Committee.* The working committee is free to frame its bye-laws. Any substantial difference of opinion will be settled by three-fourths majority, otherwise all matters will be settled unanimously. It will meet at least once a month and carry out the resolutions passed therein. It will have all the executive powers concerning land management and the planning. The working committee shall be responsible to the Sarvodaya Mandal.

The formation of Sarvodaya Mandal, the establishment of the production centre and the growing agricultural and industrial activities made it clear that the Bhoodan-Gramdan Movement has great potentialities. It is capable of generating confidence among the people and making them powerful. The non-violent approach of Vinoba is highly effective and useful. Even though the village Mangroth was facing lack of water supply specially drinking water, the people have shown remarkable progress in the field of economic development and rural uplift. They have relinquished the age-old concept of ownership of land and established new socio-economic values. The happiness of Mangroth is possible for other villages of India also. Thus the concept of Bhoodan Gramdan of Acharya Vinoba provides a non-violent solution to the socio-economic problems of the villages in India.

References

- Dhadda Siddharaj, Gramdan : The Latest Phase of Bhoodan, 1957, Kashi.
- Vinoba Bhave, Principles and Philosophy of the Bhoodan Yagna, 1976.
- Misra Raghavendra Nath, Bhoodan Movement in India : An Economic Assessment, 1972, Delhi.
- Suresh Ram, Towards a Total Revolution, 1968, Allahabad.

10

Details of Land Donation

There were 182 donations representing an area of 1,955.18 acres. Out of this 88 donations with an area of 324.82 acres proved to be ineffective due to various reasons. In the year 1969, the total effective donation was confined to 94 donors with an area of 1,630.36 acres of land. The reasons for ineffective were that in some cases the donors made declarations but did not carry them out of the total stage of donation. In some cases the donors made declarations of donation but later on requested the Bhoodan Mandal to return the land. In some cases the legal processes were completed and distributed. But the donors ejected the Bhoodan holders and were them selves possessing the land. In some cases, the donated land was uncultivable and hence remained undistributed. Out of the 25 selected villages, one village was completely eliminated from investigation because all the donations in this village proved to be ineffective. Out of the remaining 24 villages, in 15 villages the donated area was upto 50 acres. In 4 villages the donations ranged from 51 to 100 acres. In 3 villages the donations fell between 101 and 200 acres. Only in 2 villages the donations exceeded 200 acres and went up to about 400 acres. As far as the number of donors was concerned, in 18 villages the number of donors did not exceed 5 donors. In 5 villages there were 6 to 10 donors. Only in one village the number of donors came to 12. The average per village donation for 24 villages came to 67.93 acres. The village-wise number of donors and donated area is mentioned at Table-1.

Table 1: Village-wise Number of Donors and Areas Donated

District	Sl.No. of Village	Name of Village	No. of Donors	Area (in acres)
Aola	1	Khedikhurd	2	51.10
"	2	Poha	12	129.50
Amraoti	3	Mhasona	2	18.83
"	4	Pimpalkhuta	2	9.80
Bhandara	5	Jamakudo	7	23.79
"	6	Sitepur	4	32.50
"	7	Tikayatpur	1	26.00
Buldana	8	Chaldhana	2	368.52
Chanda	9	Bhadorni	3	13.00
"	10	Durgapur	-	00.00
"	11	Usrala	6	27.00
Nagpur	12	Borgaon	5	17.00
"	13	Kusumdhara	1	36.36
"	14	Tandulwani	3	23.04
Wardha	15	Barbadi	2	27.84
"	16	Dighi	6	9.46
"	17	Ratnapur	4	117.31
"	18	Tas	3	11.00
Yeotmal	19	Maregaon	8	31.20
"	20	Mitnapur	2	32.52
"	21	Rui	3	111.67
"	22	Rampur	1	99.30
"	23	Sheoni	5	61.00
"	24	Tadsawali	8	62.77
	25	Jalka	2	200.00

Out of the donors, about 93% were Hindus. So far as non-agricultural employment is concerned, out of 93 donors, 51 donors were such that nobody from their households was non-agriculturally employed at the time of donation. It means that all these households were wholly dependent on agriculture. This was the group of donors which contributed the maximum land in Bhoodan. The land contributed by these donors came to about 38 per cent of the total land contributed by all the donors. The average per donor area within this group came to about 12 acres. Of the 93 donors, about 60 per cent donors had 6 to 10 dependents in their households. The land contributed by this group alone came to about 51 per cent of the total land contributed by all the donors. The average per donor acres within this group came to about 15 acres. Out of the donations, the most number of donations had been received in the year 1956 (i.e. 39 donations) followed by the year 1955 (i.e. 22 donations). So far as the size of the land is concerned, about 66 per cent of the donors donated land between 0.1 and 9.9 acres. The land donated by these donors came to about 12 per cent of the total donated land. About 19 per cent donors donated land between 10 and 24.9 acres. The land donated by this group of donors came to about 18 per cent of the total. About 9 per cent donors donated land between 25 and 49.9 acres. The land donated by this group came to about 15 per cent of the total donated land. As far as the quality of the donated land is concerned, about 50 per cent of the land donated by about 52 per cent donors was of very low quality. The land revenue on thee lands was less than Re.0.50 per acre. On about 48 per cent land donated by about 43 per cent donors, the per-acre revenue varied between Re.0.50 and Re.0.99. This land was also of good quality. Only about 1 per cent land donated by about 5 per cent donors are somewhat good quality.

The motives of the donors in making donations are: about 30 per cent donors donated about 27 per cent land under moral or social pressure brought on them either by village leaders or by organizers of Bhoodan. About 13 per cent donors donated the land to have some material gain in future. A few donors were afraid that they might lose their land under the Land Ceiling Act and hence made the donations. Few persons donated their land which was unfit for cultivation. The remaining donors were totally convinced about the Bhoodan ideology and donated the land.

References

- Out of 94 donors, 1 donor was an institution, Gorakshan Sabha, Gondia. This donor, therefore has not been included.

11

Talks on Gita

Introduction

> "The Talks put the essence of the Gita into simple language and so bring it within the reach of the common man. They present the Gita from the standpoint of Samyayoga, so far as I have understood it. In the course of time my other services to the world may be forgotten, but I believe that Talks on the Gita will continue to give service. I say this because when I gave the Talks on the Gita, I did so in a state of Samadhi, in that state of consciousness which transcends the worlds."

Talks on Gita or (Gita-Pravachane) is a very lucid and logical interpretation of Gita, with remarkable precision. It is a record of talks (Pravachans) Vinoba gave to jail inmates in Dhule from February 1932 to June 1932, on every Sunday. It was taken down verbatim by Sane Guruji.

Vinoba has given a running commentary on all the 18 chapters of Gita but has chosen a different interpretation. Thread of discussion starts from Frustration - a means to spiritual growth, Non-conventional definition of Performance of duty (Swadhanna), Skill of Action - (Karmayoga), Inward effort - Basic parameter of Karmayoga, Action without activity - Akarma, One pointed ness of mind - Akagratha, Devotion (Bhakti) - Redefined, Pure state of mind - SamskarMukti, Self-surrender - Basis of spiritual experience, Looking for God, The Vision of the Cosmic Form, Devotion with and without Form, The Self and the Non-self, Building up and Breaking down, Completeness of Vision, Conflict Between Divine And Demonic Tendencies, Programme for the Seeker, and ends with Grace of the Lord.

These talks on Gita were given once a week in the prison at Dhule, one of the eastern districts in the state of Maharashtra where Vinoba was a political prisoner. Hardly there was a man of distinction in India who had not commented on the Gita. Vinoba was under a strong Gandhian influence and hence he worked out a different interpretation of this sacred text in line with the freedom movement that was in full swing at that time.

Yoga of Despondency

In the background of Gita is a war, between two families, ready to start. Arjuna the main hero on one side, looks at the family members, elders and friends on the other side and experiences a strong sense of frustration for infighting in the family. Although he was a great warrior, he merely broke-down by thinking on the utter futility of this war and in that moment of depression he asks his mentor about what he should do. The answer given by Shri Krishna is equally unexpected. He says your present reluctance to fight is illusion. Your problem is not regarding fight but the fight against my relatives, my brothers, my friends. Krishna says that your real fight has to be against 'I' and 'My') rather than the fight outside. It is in this context of how to come out of our ego i.e. 'I' and the result of the ego i.e. 'My' that all the seventeen chapters have been commented upon.

Self-Knowledge And Equanimity

The chapter deals with non-conventional definition of Performance of duty-Swadharma. This concept of swadharma in India of 1932 was largely interpreted as Hindu dharma or its sects and sub-sects along with the rituals and signs on the forehead, a mala or a rosary, a particular type of dress or the naming, caste and sex. Vinoba's contribution to the interpretation of swadharma is unique when he says that our swadharma comes to us with such ease and naturalness that we should cherish it without effort. But because of many kinds of illusion, this does not happen; or else, it is performed with great difficulty; or even if it is practiced, it gets corrupted with many sorts of faults.

There are many external forms assumed by the illusion but, if we examine them, only one thing is at the bottom of it all, namely, a restricted and shallow identification of one self with the body. Myself, and those related to me through the body, sets the limits of my expansion. Anyone outside this circle is to me a stranger or an enemy. This identification with the body builds a wall around me and cuts me off, and I regard only the bodies as "me" and "mine". Falling into this double trap of identification of oneself and one's people with the body we start putting up all sorts of little walls. Almost everybody is busy doing this. One man puts up an enclosure called "attachment to family" and lives in it; another builds and lives in an enclosure called “attachment to nation”. But what is the result of this ? Only one thing : the germs of base thoughts multiply, and the health which is swadharma is destroyed. The practice of swadharma or the duty towards oneself, family, society and nation is to be progressively achieved by converting the intelligence or budhi to discriminating intelligence (vivekbudhi) which is also called Wisdom or Pragna.

At the end, the qualities of the man of steadfast mind (sthitaprajna) the embodiment of self-control is described i.e. controlling the organs of perception and action (indriyas). This control is not easy. But to do as the tortoise does, drawing in its limbs in times of danger, and using them when it is safe; to draw the senses away from objects, and to use them for higher services - this discipline is difficult but can be achieved by effort. A person established in ‘Pragna’ or ‘Wisdom’ becomes more balanced or equanimous and experiences his higher self which is beyond passion, greed and arrogance.

Yoga of Action

The chapter on ‘Karma-Yoga’ or ‘Yoga of Action’ was interpreted in context of then prevailing life in India People in towns and villages were in high state of inactivity. Many of them had taken to addiction to tobacco opium or country liquor. Men were most of the time gossiping, and most of the manual work was thrust upon women. In the name of religion high class Hindus had developed a strong dislike towards poor members of society and were treating women as second class citizens. In large cities, men had taken to English education and life style as the highest aim of life. Manual work was to be avoided and white collar generation came into significant existence. People became 'intellectuals' rather than intelligent. There was 'inactivity' in villages and 'fruitless activity in cities'. In this context, he again draws the attention of Hindu society that Gita is not for Sanyasis but for House-holders and swadharma is to act. Dignity of labour and maintaining health by simple natural means was already established by his mentor Gandhi as a part of swadharma. Vinoba further adds to the list the concept of 'bhavana' or 'love' as important ingredients of work.

Work has to be done for maintaining health, tilling and harvesting of land or craftsmanship of an artisan or merchandising of goods by merchants etc. All this should be directed towards growth of soul by adding love and earning money by fair means in return for work as a house-holder is expected to do. As he illustrates this chapter, he says that 'result of karma-yogi's (skilful worker) action is that while his life goes on smoothly, his body and mind are radiant; and society too prospers. Besides these two benefits, he also receives the great gift of 'chitta-shudhi' or purity of mind ....,The Karma Yogi's work is a form of prayer (japa). His mind is purified by it, and the clear mind receives the image of 'jnana' or 'true knowledge'.

Illustrating this concept further, he gives example of Sena the barber. As he cleaned other people's heads wisdom came to him, 'Look, I remove the dirt from other's heads, but have I ever removed the dirt from my own head, from my own mind?' The language of the spirit came to him through his work. Again he says that as we weed the field, the karma-yogi (skilful worker) gets the idea of removing the weeds of habit and passion from his heart. He concludes that karma-yogi acting thus, through the terms of his own trade or occupation gains knowledge of perfection.

Vikarma - The Key to Karma - Yoga

This Chapter brings in another new concept of 'Vikarma' or Inward Effort as the key to Yoga of action. Without this key the lock of ultimate purity or self-knowledge will not and cannot open. This state has been defined as 'Desirelessness', It is a quality of mind. As a means of creating this, the pursuit of 'Swadharma' is not enough, other aids are needed. For this, we need to purify the mind. By self-examination, we have to cleanse the mind of its dirt. When 'Vikarma' or the action of the mind and heart enters into 'Karma' or outward action desirelessness (purity) grows within us little by little. Without inward effort he illustrates a case of social worker like this 'To serve people who are poor or lame or are unhappy and in difficulties and to make them happy is the duty that falls to us in the ordinary course'. But we should not conclude, therefore, that all social workers have become karma-yogis. If the attitude of mind (bhavana) in social service is not pure it can become a terrifying thing. If the outward action is not moistened by the heart's affection then the performance of swadharma would remain barren, it would not bear the flower and the fruit of 'desirelessness'. Moreover, where the heart is not engaged egoism too would show its head. Sick men are usually peevish - and those who nurse them without the true spirit of service will only be disgusted.

When the inner feeling goes with the action, the latter is transformed into something unique. The power that karma develops at the touch of vikarma is indescribable. The infinite power of the practice of swadharma lies latent. Touch it with vikarma, and see what work it can do! In the resulting explosion desire and anger are destroyed, and the way made clear for the attainment of supreme wisdom. When you apply vikarma to karma, the latter begins to acquire divine radiance. The mother strokes her child's back. A hand moves up and down a back, and no more. But who can describe the feelings arising in the hearts of the mother and the child from this commonplace action?

What do we mean by saying that, by pouring vikarma into karma, it becomes akarma. If we mean that, while acting, we seem not to act, we do not feel the burden of action. Though we act, we are not the doer. By vikarma, by inner purity, karma ceases to be karma. An action performed with pure heart does not attach itself to us. It leaves no residue of sin or virtue, paap or punya; else, what a heavy pressure of action would our hearts and minds have to bear! We feel that action crowds in on us from all sides, we feel that it has caught us by the throat. Just as the waves of the sea dash with force against the land and make channels into it, the complexity of action (karma) enters the mind and agitates it. The quality of pleasure and pain, sukh and dukh, develops; all peace is lost. The action takes place and is over, but its force remains behind. Action corrupts the mind, and destroys sleep. But if, with karma we combine vikarma, then, however much work you do; you will not feel its strain. The mind becomes still steady and radiant, like the polestar. Saints, though engaged in a thousand action, do not allow a ripple to arise in the still waters of their mind. One can never understand this miracle until one goes to a saint and sees it. Though surrounded by libraries and reading rooms, man everywhere still remains a monkey without culture or knowledge. Though knowledge spreads so rapidly, how does man's mind manage to remain still empty? One man says that human memory is getting weaker; another, that men are losing the power of concentration. Lord Krishna said to Arjuna, 'You have been listening to so far too may things, and your mind is dazed. Till it gets steady, you will not see the way clearly. Stop reading books and listening to people, and now take sanctuary with the saints. There you can read the book of life. There, silent speech clears all your doubts. By going there you will understand how utterly serene the mind can be while performing continuous service; you will understand how, though action rages without, the heart can be turned to produce unbroken music.

The Two Aspects of Akarma - Yoga & Sanyasa

Vinoba spent several years to absorb this chapter which he considers key to the whole Gita. Summary of his deep study is the final goal of yoga and Sanyasa 'Action without activity'. These two traditions of spiritual seekers in India-large majority of house-holders engaged in social and economic activity and making themselves fitter for experience by constantly adding inward effort of purity to their external work and a minority group who do not get married and consequently cut themselves off from social and economic activity, get absorbed mainly in inward effort doing minimum external work to keep life going. Both these groups ultimately come to the same result. 'Action without fatigue, without stress with very high value adding power, power which move mountains, revolutionise societies - Power of Buddha, Jesus or Gandhi.' Although both traditions lead to same result, the path of action is preferred because it is safe. Indian History has many actual examples of men who got the results of self-realisation in this way. Potters, weavers, merchants and kings who reached the goal in this way are illustrated in it. Vinoba explains that external actions reveal the real quality of our minds by explaining the beauty and spiritual purpose of action. He says a man becomes angry because anger was within and external action created circumstances by which it came out. If we do not act, we cannot test our mind that it has anger, jealousy, hatred etc. Our action talks. Our action is a mirror which shows us our true form. When we act and discover our own defects, we are impelled to employ 'Vikarma' or inward action to remove them. When actions do not distort the mind, when it becomes natural and normal (sahaja), it becomes 'Akarma' - action with intense results. Example of Sun is taken to illustrate this final result - 'Akarma' - the goal of all spiritual practices. It shines, gives life to the whole world. As sun rises, people get ready for work, birds start coming out of nest, but Sun is just shining, it is normal and natural for Sun to shine. All activity is inspired by his presence but still he is the witness. Doing nothing though doing all things, to do all things by doing nothing, both alike are 'Yoga'. However to reach the goal of doing nothing by doing all things - the path of Karma-Yoga - Yoga of Action is to be preferred, because it is both the way and the goal - where the path ends, goal is there. There is room in Karma yoga for effort and practice. Through this path of action, one can learn to control the senses little by little. Ease in practice distinguishes 'karma yoga ' or the path of action from 'sanyasa' path of renunciation but in the state of perfection, both are the same. This is 'Akarma ' action without activity

Controlling the Mind

This Chapter deals with the technique of meditation. He points out three important parameters to obtain the result, one is one-pointed ness of mind, second is setting bounds to one's life to achieve this and third is evenness of vision or a state of equanimity. For achieving this we need practice and objective outlook towards family, society, nation and the world. One-pointed ness can be achieved by stopping the wheel of thoughts in the mind by coming out of the habit of brooding on trifles. If the mind incessantly (?) keeps on moving, the man's whole strength is lost. There is no kind of discipline. Our actions should be progressively purer by adopting the technique of Karma and Vikarma. To support the concentrated state of mind, he says that 'Let us turn away not only from bad things, but also from excess of even goods things'. Such disciplined conduct is called 'setting bounds to life'. Third parameter is a balanced outlook. So long as we cannot experience that the whole creation is auspicious, the mind will not be one-pointed. As long as we think that some-thing is wrong with the world, we look at all things with suspicion. If one looks at the world with friendly eyes, a perennial stream will spring in the heart, divine stars will shine in the inner firmament. He sums the chapter by concluding remarks like this - For dhyana-yoga (the way of meditation), it is thus seen that one-pointed ness of mind, disciplined living and a friendly and balanced outlook are necessary. Besides these, two other aids, detachment and practice, are mentioned. The first is a negative, destructive method, the other, positive and constructive. To uproot and throw away the weeds from the field is destructive work and this is vairagya detachment. To sow seeds in the field is constructive work. To think good thoughts again and again is abhyasa - practice. vairagya is negative, abhyasa is positive.

Surrender to God

Vinoba explains in this chapter about the anger of the angry man, the love of the lover, the agony of the sufferer, happiness of the happy one, the drowsiness of the idler, the activity of the worker, all these have an in-built divinity in them. He shows that man's pleasure hunt is because there is no joy in his life and this condition in turn is because he is unable to experience divinity in ordinary things of life as taught by Gita. Once we have seen the true nature of the universe and tasted its joy, we shall find these other pleasures insipid. The best way to discover this joy is 'Bhakti' or Devotion. Even if we have to beg, there is greatness in begging from the God rather than from the world and this begging is Bhakti. Citing his own version of Devotion he says, 'If on seeing the great rivers, if one can feel the river as compassion of God flowing before us, such a man is a true devotee'. If man's heart-beat leaps at the sight of the rain-bow, dances at the sight of the daffodils, he is a true devotee. It starts with desire or 'Sakam Bhakti' and ends with joy without external stimulation which Gita calls 'Nishkam Bhakti' or end of all material desires. Describing three kinds of Bhaktas, Gita says first kind looks at the whole world through eyes of love, the second kind through the eye of discovery, and the third from the point of view of the world's welfare. There is also a fourth type of perfect devotee. His method is to see God in the ugly as in the handsome, in the beggar as in the king, in men, women, animals and birds, everywhere he sees the presence of God. This pure devotee sees the grandeur of God in majestic ocean, the mother like tenderness of God in cow, in the earth he sees His presence, in the clear sky His purity, in Sun, Moon and Stars, His brightness and beauty, His softness in flowers, and in the evil man the God who tests and tries us. Thus he practices the art of seeing the one God at play everywhere and in doing so, one day the seer-saint merges into the Lord. This was what Vinoba understood as devotion with all its variegated tools and this is the result of surrendering one's ego to God.

Achieving the Goal

In this chapter, Vinoba says that the purity of existence can get in tune with God during and at the end of the life. 'Eating, drinking, sitting, sleeping, wandering, a little work...likes and dislikes, honour and dishonour, pain and pleasure in endless variety! And they all leave associations, impacts and build up tendencies in the mind. Life is an aggregate of 'Sanskaras' or tendencies. Important and distinct actions leave a deep impression on the mind; and other actions fade away from memory. However, a single powerful 'sanskara' alone remains at last as the essential thing. All the efforts of life should be guided by the idea that this final fruit should be full of sweetness, that the last moment should be blissful. When the end is sweet, all else is sweet.

In order to achieve this, we should aim to conquer the fear of death. Thinking of death - not brooding over it - is a means of avoiding sin. With constant awareness of death, with what strength can man commit sin? Man has become so frightened of death that he cannot bear ever the thought of it. Only thing which consoles us for our miseries is diversion, and yet this is the greatest of our miseries. For it is this which makes us ruin ourselves. Diversion amuses us and leads us unconsciously to death. Therefore remembering that death is the crown of life, we should constantly practice the means by which we can make our last moments holy, pure and sweet. To create such good 'sanskara', let noble thoughts course through the mind. Let the hands be busy doing deeds of goodness. Thoughts of God within, and the performance of Swadharma without, these should go on constantly. When the hands perform acts of service till the last breath, the full moon of Bhavana shines brightly, the mind's sky is free from desire, and the intellect is bright and keen - when a man dies in this state, we may take it that he has merged in God. In order to make such an auspicious ending, one must watch day and night and wage skilful war. Not even for an instant, should an evil tendency be permitted in the mind. And in order to gain strength necessary for this, one should remember His name, and meditate on His truth.

The Yoga of Dedication

In this chapter Vinoba described the rare power of the name of God. There is an art in chanting this name and experience gained thereby is beyond words and that is why it is sweet. Though this knowledge is a hidden secret, Lord Krishna opens it out for all to understand with ease. The Gita is the twice-distilled essence of the Vedic Dharma and the name of the Lord is the essence of the Vedas. It is certain that through 'Ramnama' one can attain 'moksha' which means that moksha becomes easy for women, children, the rustic and the poor, the weak, sick, lame and indeed for everyone. In whatever action, the man is engaged, through that natural action alone he is able to reach supreme by considering every human form as manifestation of God - such is this method. Another aspect is to dedicate whatever we do to him. Relate to him every act of yours.

There is no question of fitness - no pre-qualification. Any body who does this with pure heart gets the result. When learned men who say 'I'. 'I' are left behind, innocent and devout women go forward. When the mind is pure and heart full of simplicity and holiness, moksha or liberation is not difficult to attain. If the action is filled with pure 'bhavana', with the attitude of service, it becomes 'yagna'-dedication. The essence of practice is to dissolve our Ego at the feet of the Lord by dedicating our base tendencies like lust, greed, anger etc. with sincere heart and we become pure as a result. Our senses are no longer our enemies. Their power for good is boundless. Therefore the best and the noblest way to use every one of the senses with the intellect surrendered to the Lord.This is called 'Raja-Yoga'. How pure and holy the food will be when it is cooked with the 'bhavana' of pleasing the Lord. The moments of our daily life may appear commonplace, but in reality they are not so, they carry enormous significance. Life is dark, ugly and full of sorrow. But just for a while, let the mind consider that all our actions are for the sake of the Lord. Then we will realise how full of beauty and value our lives become. Do not say what good can the word 'Rama' do. Just try saying it and see what happens.

Creation is but a mirror. What you are and what you bring to this mirror, the image of this, you see in this world. Therefore approach all creation with the feeling that it is good - that it is pure. Carry the same 'attitude' to all your ordinary actions. Then you will see a miraculous change. If you have the 'bhavana' that Lord is always by your side, then you, His servant will know no fear even if the whole world turns up-side down. Therefore turn your heart towards God. Attain his grace. Dedicate all actions to Him. Become altogether His. If you strengthen the attitude that all actions should be offered up to the Lord, this sordid life will become divine, the commonplace will become beautiful. Such actions are not illogical but beyond logic. Where logic ends, spirituality begins.

Looking for God

Vinoba in this Chapter takes the example of child learning alphabet - big letters first and as the practice develops make the same letters small and recognise them. Alternatively easy letters first and complex after a little practice. The immense being which we see in the ocean is also present in the little drop of water. God who is in 'Rama' is also in 'Ravana', what is found in the gross is present in the subtle. What is found in the simple, is also in the complex. This vast creation is God's book. In this book of creation, God is written down everywhere in beautiful letters. But we do not understand it. It is this sick mind that stands as an obstacle to our seeing God. It is essential to get rid of this state of mind. Hence because our minds are sick, let us experience God in our father, mother, Guru, a saint, pure children like Dhruva and Prahalada. After one learns to see God in serene and holy human forms, then we turn our eyes to sublime and beautiful aspects of nature. Beauty of sunrise and sunset, this art divine -lovely and majestic waters of Ganges which carries away in her course all the uncleanliness of our mind and body, wind the messenger of God whispering in our heart, fire which burns our impurities etc. We now look to God in creatures, cow full of tenderness and love, the swiftness of horse, majesty of lion, cleanliness of serpent.

Now turn to couples - love of father and son, mother and child, love of brothers, love of husband and wife, love between Rama and monkeys 'Nara and Vanara'. Then the birds majestic peacock with thousand eyes and many coloured brightness in its feather, sweet melodious voice of cuckoo and great municipal service of nature in crow. We just think of fables of Aesop based on child's lively interest in objects of creation. In it, foxes, dogs, crows, deer, hares, tortoise, snakes, worms all talk and laugh. The truth of the matter is that God is present in all the forms of creation. As holy rivers, mighty mountains, the majestic ocean, the tender-hearted cow, the noble steed, the magnificent lion, the sweet voiced cuckoo, the beautiful peacock, the pure hermit snake, the crow flapping its wings, the restless flame, the still stars - in all this; He is present. Gross and subtle, pure and mixed simple and complex - learn all this and realise in the end that there is no place where God is not. In every atom, He alone is present. From the ant to the universe, He spreads. The Lord who cares equally for all, the compassionate one who is all knowledge, tenderness, skill, holiness and beauty - He stands on all sides everywhere.

The Vision of the Cosmic Form

In this chapter the Lord reveals His visible form and so His Grace. Arjuna said "Lord, I wish behold with these eyes your complete form, the form in which is manifest all the power of your glory". What he really prayed for was the vision of cosmic form was to see all at once the Omnipresent Lord, who pervaded all time past, present and future and all space here, above, below and everywhere.

Vinoba says verses describing the cosmic form of God cannot be commented. We can only recite the verses describing it and cleanse the mind of sin, purify it only at one point Lords tells Arjuna that this cosmic form cannot be grasped permanently until you dissolve the Ego and become the instrument in the hands of God for all your actions. To achieve this, the qualifying characteristics are: "He who bears enmity towards none, he who stands impartial and is free from attachment, and serves me selflessly, he who dedicates to me all that he does, he who is filled with devotion to me, all enduring, free of passion and desire, full of love, such a devotee becomes an instrument in the hands of the Lord, This is the essence of Gita's teaching."

Devotion with and without Form

In this chapter, Arjuna asks the question that there are two types of devotees - one who worship the image to grasp and experience spiritual thought and the other grasp the thought directly and act accordingly in search of an experience. Which of the two is better? Vinoba explains that question of Arjuna is similar to asking the mother - which of your two sons are dearer to you? What can the poor mother reply? If at all a reply is pressed for, she would say the younger son because he needs the presence of mother more than the elder one. Similar answer is given by Shri Krishna that if at all answer is needed, one with form is closer to me.

Vinoba further illustrated this by referring to the famous epic 'Ramayana'. When Rama is going to the forest for fourteen years, his younger brother Laxman pleads that he too wants to accompany him. When Rama dissuades him not to do so by an argument, Laxman puts stop to the argument like this 'O Rama I have grown up nourished by your love. I am only a child. I cannot bear the burden of living here without you.' He accompanies Rama for 14 years. This is worship with form or image. However, Tulsidasji describes that when Rama left for forest, Bharat his other younger brother was not in Ayodhya. When he reached home, his father had died and Royal Guru Vashishtha advises him to assume the rule of the state. But Bharata answers that 'first I must see Rama before I decide this question'. He makes arrangements for running the administration. His line of thinking is 'Kingdom belongs to Rama. To arrange for the administration is like doing Rama's work. Devotion to Rama means carrying out his work; else what good is the devotion?' This is the devotion without form. This classical example of Formless Devotion ends with following dialogue between the brothers. Bharat says, 'Rama my Lord, I shall humbly do your bidding. Whatever you say, I shall not doubt or question'. But as he prepares to leave, he turns to Rama and says, 'Sir, my heart is yet unreconciled. I feel as if I have lost something'. Rama at once understood his yearning and gave him one of his personal effects as symbol in place of Rama. Though Bharata was firm in his loyalty to duty and principle, he too needed the living warmth of the symbol. This is Devotion without Form.

The chapter ends with following words from Shree Krishna 'Arjuna, it does not matter whether you are devotee with or without form. More important is to become a devotee with all your heart'.

The Self and the Non-self

The most important aid to Swadharma-a discriminating insight - to separate the bran from the wheat or smelting gold from the ore - is discussed and the steps are shown how to get the gold and remove the impurities. For this Vinoba gives the example of Coconut where the hard exterior shell is to be broken to reach and taste the pulp. Similarly to taste the sweet juicy pulp of jack-fruit, the rough sharp exterior has to be carefully removed. There is a clear message here for inward journey. One must understand that 'I' am altogether distinct from the body, separate entirely beautiful, bright, holy and free from even a trace of imperfection. As we proceed inward the self illuminates the body and puts joy, power, fearlessness self-control etc. As we move inwards, attachment to the body slowly decreases, one experiences genuine freedom and power. No true safety is possible so long as there is attachment to body and consequent fear.

In this inward journey, we progressively experience God - first as an impartial witness. When the life of morality begins, He encourages us when good things take place through us. When the devotee discovers that his own efforts are inadequate to cleanse the subtle impurities of his mind, when he is on the point of break-down, He becomes the Helper of the helpless and rushes to his aid. After that we see that He also is the enjoyer of the fruit of action. His presence only makes us experience the sweetness of the fruit. From this point we start experiencing our divinity. When our ego surrenders totally to the inner self- the inner master - we reach the ultimate goal. During this long, arduous, at times risky and dangerous inner journey, the tools which are helpful and therefore essential are action and devotion ultimately blending into action with devotion. Vinoba says to achieve this firm foundation of morality is indispensable. We should discriminate between essential and non-essential and hold fast to the essential. This discriminating experience which is called 'jnana' or realisation should pervade every fibre of our body. It should flow through one's heart. It should express itself through the hands and the feet, the eyes and the ears. One should attain a state when all the organs of perception and action work with this consciousness. Our symptoms of this realisation have been narrated by twenty virtues like humility, sincerity, non-violence, straightforwardness, forgiveness etc. The substance is that we should make our lives grow more and more by distinguishing the body from the spirit and thus feel ourselves with the presence of God within.

Building-up and Breaking-down

This chapter briefly deals about Self and the Non-self. Entire material body including mind-intellect consciousness and ego-system consists of subtle particles and electrical charges broadly divided into Gross called Tamas. Subtle called - Rajas and subtler one called sattva or pure manifestation. These three modes of nature are called Gunas. Chief characteristic of Tamas is Laziness - inability to do anything fruitful. It is an enemy which destroys peace and happiness of individual and society. Laziness corrupts every one from the lowest to the highest. When the body is lazy, the mind and the intellect are lazy too. Under the effect of Tamas (Laziness), men grow rusty and useless; the limbs and senses of the rich are eaten with rust because they are never used.

Educated and intelligent men become victims of various diseases because under the effect of Tamas, they never do any physical work. To shake off laziness, one must perform bodily labour. This is the only way to conquer laziness. If we fail to do this, we cannot but receive due punishment from Nature. We have to endure it in the form of sickness and other miseries. The time spent on the bodily labour is not wasted. It does yield result. We have sound health. Our minds become bright and keen and pure. This is one of the methods to overcome the Tamas or Laziness. Chief characteristic of Rajas or hyper-activity is desire to do all sorts of things - a limitless desire for action with all consuming greed. As a result, we are unable to control the rush of our instincts and passions. Another sign of Rajas is absence of steadiness. The man of Rajas is ever busy taking up and abandoning things. All actions under its effect are restless and uncertain. The way to come out of restlessness is to combine action with inward effort. This results in inner purity. Keep on acting constantly and surrender the fruit of action to God. Acting this way, slowly Rajas is destroyed. It is necessary to destroy this demon of every rising greed and desires. This is the Karma-yoga of Gita. If these two are conquered, we are left with Satva or a pure state of our existence - peaceful and bright, full of creative energy. However, even this is to be conquered not by killing but by wounding. Constantly making an effort to remain in this state, it becomes our nature to remain pure. Pride of purity slowly goes away. Any negligence by the seeker due to pride in this state, is likely to drag him down to the state of hyper-activity and further down to laziness. Constant vigilance till it becomes our nature to remain pure is an absolute necessity of this state. Thereafter, the seeker tries to cross-over the material self consisting of all these three modifications. The tool here is to seek His grace with all the heart. It does come. Having reached this state, no further effort is required to remain pure.

Completeness of Vision

In this chapter, all the ideas of the Gita find their fulfillment. Shri Krishna calls this particular Chapter 'Shashtra'- a scripture because in this chapter science and philosophy of life that have been taught till now find completion. The function of Vedas is to awaken in man awareness of his own power to know everything, guide everything. This is called 'Parmartha': Because this is done in this chapter it has been called 'Vedasaara' the essence of the Veda. In the last chapter, Shri Krishna says that for Self-realisation, Bhakti is the ultimate tool; without it realisation is not possible. This chapter starts with the description of the world as mighty tree with huge branches nourished by three 'gunas'. This tree is to be cut with the axe of desirelessness and detachment. With Bhakti or devotion this effort becomes easy. This devotion is a blend of action, love, and knowledge. All difficulties on the path of realisation get converted to pleasure with the touch of this devotion.

Differentiated concept of Purushottama - the Supreme Self which Sri Krishna is, the individual self which is non-perishable and has to be realised and tools of Bhakti or devotion which are perishable are dealt with here. There is deep significance in the perishable nature of the tools. This is not the fault of the creation; it is its glory. Because of this, creation is ever new. Yesterday's flowers will not do for to-day's worship. New flowers are required and are available. In the same way new bodies will be provided every now and then to give freshness and life to the worship. Because the body is transient, it is beautiful. Because the instruments are ever new, the enthusiasm for worship grows; the habit of service develops. This is the essence of 'Bhakti' or devotion. This conceptual reality of Purushottama or Supreme Self to whom our ego can surrender so that purusha or self within us can awaken and ultimately be realised. The ever new, ever changing tool of worship is a necessity from the beginning to the end of the path. However worship does not mean only offering flowers and consecrated rice or Vermillion (Kumkum). This is there but it is to be supported by our day-to-day actions. To keep house-hold utensils clean and polished is a worship. To clean a lamp is also a worship. To whet the scythe and make it ready for reaping is a worship. To lubricate the rusty hinge of the door, is worship too. All our actions from morning to evening - all are worship of the God. To a king of scriptures like Gita, a daily half our worship or puja yields no satisfaction. Its keen desire is that the whole of life should be filled with the Lord and be a form worship. And this worship is to surrender our 'I' at the feet of Supreme reality 'Purshottama' so that we ultimately transform ourselves from perishable to imperishable 'Self- the 'Purusha'.

The conflict between Divine and Demon

This chapter describes the qualities needed to be perfected in the life of accomplished seeker and also describes the darkness with which seeker has to fight before getting established. In essence it describes the conflict between the divine and the demonic qualities. Kurukshetra is both outside us and within us. When we observe it carefully, it is the battle raging within that we see assuming shape in the world without. To speak the truth, the battle is only within ourselves. As there are good qualities on one side and bad qualities on the other, both the armies are well arranged. Commander of good qualities is 'abhaya' or fearlessness. Fearlessness has been given first place in a long list of twenty-six qualities. This is not an accident. In an atmosphere charged with fear, good qualities cannot grow. While in front fearlessness stands alert, humility guards the rear. This is an excellent arrangement. If we have first twenty five qualities mentioned in this chapter but no humility, 'ahamkar' or Ego principle will attack the army from the back and destroy it. In the absence of humility, there is no knowing when victory will turn into defeat. Osther qualities between fearlessness and humility are compassion, tenderness, forgiveness, serenity, patience, non-violence, loyalty etc. On the other side, there is an army of ignorance, vanity, power and wealth. Under the effect of these negative qualities, one says that 'I am the only person fit to hold all the wealth of the world. The whole world should come under my control'. Desire, anger and greed are the sources from where negative qualities multiply. Way out is the control of the senses. This is the path laid down by 'Shashtras'. 'Shashtras' are made up of the experience of the saints gained through their efforts. Hence to overcome negativities, 'Self-control' as advised by 'Shashtras' is inevitable. Waging this incessant war between divine and demonic qualities, there may be temporary defeats in the battle but in the end, war is won by the divine qualities. Hence doing good to the world is to show the man-kind the pure and beautiful path of virtue. Thus demonstrating victory of divine over the evil forces.

Programme for the Seeker

Vinoba says that only when our life proceeds within bounds and in an accepted, disciplined way that the mind can be free. The Sun is free and independent. He is regular. It is in this regularity that the essence of his freedom lies. Hence in this chapter Shri Krishna sets down a programme of action. The programme of Yagna (Regeneration), Dana (Sharing with society) & Tapa (purification of body and mind) is described as the debt to the nature. Nature is pure and it is polluted by human beings; hence we have to regenerate by yagna (Regeneration). Regeneration is to replenish loss, and to purify things. Society has supported a part of our existence; we have to repay the debt. Dana

(Charity) for various social purposes is repaying the debt. Rays of Sun in summer destroy plenty of morbid matter on the earth and purify saline water of the sea to provide sweet water through rain. This is tapa which is also yagna or regeneration by removing or destroying impurities. In fact three orders of nature, society and the body are not distinct. Society is not outside creation and not so the body. The creative effort we make, charity we give and japas we perform, all these can be called Yagna in the comprehensive sense. There is no question of receiving any fruit because we have already received this. What we have taken, we must now return. Through yagna (regeneration), we maintain equilibrium in nature, through dana (charity) in society and tapa (purification) in the body. Again Yagna, Dana and Tapa are divided into 'Satvik', 'Rajasik' and 'Tamasik'. If there is expectation of fruit in Yagna it is Rajavik; if it is fruitless it is Tamasik. Disorderly actions become lifeless. Into such actions Tamas enters. Through it, no noble thing can be created. From it no fruit will grow. Even though there is no desire for fruit in performing 'yagna', it ought to yield noble fruit. In this way, fruitful action purifies our mind and heart, same classification applies to Dana (charity) and Tapa (purity). When it is fruitful, it leads to Beauty & Grace which is the result of purity.

Grace of God

In this chapter, no new concepts are introduced and only whatever we have learnt is being concluded. First thing we learnt in Gita is that we have to act - keep on acting but surrender the fruit of our actions to God. These actions are of three types Satvic - which bring noble fruit, Rajasic - which gives mixed fruit of pleasure and pain, and Tamasic or fruitless activity / activity which bears painful fruit. Out of this, Shri Krishna advises that fruitless activity should be totally curbed and mixed fruit activity to be progressively purified by surrendering its fruit to God. Resultant Satvic activity has also some defects, but this should not be given up. As inward purity grows, the effort in the action becomes less. From effort to gentleness, from gentleness to subtlety, from subtlety to nothingness, the activity tends to zero and action towards infinity. After having said this, Sri Krishna tells Arjuna, 'You have heard with attention, all that I have been saying. Consider my words fully and do what you think right'. Thus Shri Krishna generously sets Arjuna free. In the same breath, in the next verse he says, 'Arjuna, give up everything and take refuge in Me'. What does this mean? It means as long as there is Ego, there is danger in becoming free; let not any desire of your own arise in your heart. Be an observer of all the waves of desire. 'Not my, but HIS Will' - 'Not my but His Will'. "I" am not, "He" is. As you learn to subdue your ego thus, your 'Rajasic action will become pure and what will be left will be infinite action without the 'doer'. Every action coming from God - making one a vehicle of His 'divine will' No 'I', No 'My' - all His. Starting with 'I' and frustration leading to no activity in the first chapter to destroying the illusion of 'I' in the second chapter, Gita progresses to the way of action, inward action to support outward action, leading to state of egoless activity in fifth chapter. Rest of the chapters mention the tools of concentration, devotion, surrender, cosmic vision etc. to support ego less activity, and last comes total surrender to obtain His Grace which is the final tool. 'His grace having been established, no effort is needed to remain pure'. Purity becomes not only our second nature, but it becomes our first nature, our nature itself. This is the aim and end of Bhagvat-Gita.

References

❑ Vinoba Bhave, Talks on Gita, Sarva Seva Sangh, Rajghat, Varanasi, India.

12

Vinoba - True Saint of Freedom Struggle

Vinoba Bhave's contribution towards freedom movement is most unique in the annals of our sub-continent. Born in a middle class brahmin family, after doing his schooling, he has shown no interest in the college education and joined Mahatma's ashram instead as one of his ardent devotee. Vinoba's sincerity and devotion attracted Gandhiji so much that he selected Vinoba as the first Satyagrahi during the individual Satyagraha in 1940. Gandhiji has once explained why he has chosen Vinoba as the first Satyagrahi. It is impossible to improve on that thumb-nail sketch. But it may not be inappropriate to add a few more facts about his busy life, in which all the twenty-four hours of the day have been given to activity of prayerful service which alone, in his opinion, can take one to self-realization.

Vinoba has translated his principles into practice, pressed all his philosophy and mathematics in to the aid of the constructive programme which he always believed to be the external symbol of non-violence. He has trained so many students in khadi making. Vinoba was an ideal spinner, both on the wheel and the takli and with both the left and the right hands. He has produced the Marathi version of Gita. He also found time to study the Quran while carrying on in the village of Pavnar. It was a great honour that he has come to being the first Satyagrahi in a campaign that Gandhiji will strive to make the most unsullied from the point of view of non-violence. To be chosen for the honour is a great thing to have been chosen without having ever desired it is greater still.

Vinoba made his first speech at Paunar on 17th October, 1940. However the Government did not arrest him. He continued repeating his speeches on the subsequent days at Surgaon, Seloo and Deoli. It was only on the fourth day that he was arrested and sentenced to three months simple imprisonment. The following are the gist of Vinoba's statement before the District Court in Wardha on being charged with anti-war propaganda:

> "I plead guilty to the charge that I have propagated against the War in my speeches. I have done it with full understanding and with the purpose. I, however, do not agree that I have committed any crime. In fact, I regard it as my sacred duty. I have full faith in non-violence and I have spent most of my life in various constructive activities like Khadi, communal unity, service of the Harijans, basic education through crafts, and cow protection, which are based on non-violence. If a person like me takes upon himself the responsibility of offering satyagraha against the Government in this delicate situation, it is only because the regards it as his inescapable and pious duty.

Vinoba, after his release from the jail, offered Satyagraha again. This time he was sentenced to six months imprisonment. During the third time when he offered Satyagraha, the Government sent him to jail for full one year at Nagpur. The jail authorities were so reasonable to provide him with the necessary amenities permitted under the rules. He was given the type of food as per his wish and allowed to take with him books for study. They have arranged a special light for reading purposes. After his release from the Nagpur jail, Vinoba got himself engaged in the constructive work. He also toured South India in the early 1942 in connection with Hindi Prachar Movement. When Mahatma Gandhiji gave a call for the commencement of "Quit India Movement", Vinoba once again offered his services. He was arrested again and was kept in Wardha, Nagpur, Vellore and Seoni Jails. On entering the Wardha jail, Vinoba told the jailor : I have had my food for the day, and from tomorrow morning I go on an indefinite fast." The jailor was so shocked that he had committed serious mistake and asked him what was the reason for that. Vinoba told the jailor "Nothing in connection with your jail, Gandhiji had decided to begin fast soon after his arrest and I shared his decision."

During the detention period at Vellore, Vinoba spent most of the time in spinning and the study of four languages Tamil, Telugu, Kannada and Malayalam. Vinoba also delivered a series of lectures on the Gita for the benefit of the other political prisoners at Vellore. Once Vinoba wanted to write a letter to Mahatma, however the jail authorities at Vellore did not allow him to do so because Mahatma was not related to him. Vinoba therefore informed the Jail Superintendent: "I have no other relation who is so intimately connected with me as Mahatma Gandhi. If I am not allowed to write to him, I shall not write to anybody else." And so, Vinoba did not write any letter to any body for the full term of his detention. Vinoba was released from the Seoni jail in early May, 1944. He returned straight to Wardha and rejoined his creative work first at Gopuri. He started a community kitchen as an experiment in Samya-Yoga or Sarvodaya. After that he left Pavnar.

Mahatma Gandhiji has passed over both Patel and Nehru to choose him to lead civil resistance against the British. But Vinoba had been long demobilized and was on the verge of being walled up in the Gandhian epoch. Vinoba had been pretty well prepared for the job. Rebellion and self-sacrifice are in his blood. He believes India needs a great diffusion of small machines and a more decentralized system of production, based on the village, not the city. Planning must start with putting people to work, not machines. His gospel of self-help often upsets his hearers. Open-minded as a teacher, Vinoba draws upon practical farming and prayer about equally in formulating his doctrine. Though met everywhere by passionate education, he remains free of both delusions of grandeur and pride of poverty.

The jails for Vinoba had become the places of reading and writing. He saw the proofs of his book 'Gitai' (Marathi translation of Gita) in the Dhulia jail. Lectures given by him on Gita to the colleagues in the Dhulia jail collected by Sane Guruji were later published as a book. Writing of the book "Swarajya Shastra" (the treatise of self rule) and the collection of the bhajans (religious songs) of the saint Gyaneshwar, Eknath and Namdev were completed. In Nagpur jail, 'Ishavasyavritti' and 'Sthitaprajna Darshan' were written in the Seoni jail. Four languages of the South India were learnt by Vinoba at Vellore jail and the script of Lok Nagari was also created here after research. His writings covering diverse areas of religion, philosophy, education and Sarvi are thought provoking and yet accessible to the common people. The popularity of his writings has proved his ability to relate to the people. The competence of this multi-lingual scholar as an editor was also of high order as displayed by his editing of 'Maharashtra Dharma' (mentioned earlier), Sarvodaya(in Hindi) and Sevak(in Marathi).

In March 1948, Gandhi's followers and constructive workers met at Sevagram. The idea of Sarvodaya Samaj (society) surfaced and started getting acceptance. Vinoba got busy with activities which would sooth the wounds of the partition of the nation. In the beginning of 1950, he launched the programme of kanchan-mukti (freedom from dependence on gold, i.e. money) and Rishi-Kheti (cultivation without the use of bullocks as was practiced by Rishis, i.e. the sages of ancient times). In April 1951, after attending the Sarvodaya conference at Shivrampalli, he started his peace-trek on foot through the violence-torn region of Telangana(now in Andhra Pradesh). The disturbances were caused by the communists. On April 18, 1951, his meeting with the villagers at Pochampalli opened a new chapter in the history of non-violent struggle. The Harijans of the village told him that they needed 80 acres of land to make a living. Referring to this, Vinoba asked the villagers if they could do something to solve this problem. To everybody's surprise, Ram Chandra Reddy, a landlord, got up and showed his willingness to give 100 acres of land. This incident, unplanned and unheard, showed a way to solve the problem of the landless. The Bhoodan(Gift of the Land)movement was launched.

The response to the movement was spontaneous. In Telangana, the gift of land averaged 200 acres of land per day. On the journey from Paunar to Delhi, the average gift was 300 acres a day. Vinoba had put five crore acre as the target. While walking in Uttar Pradesh in May 1952, Vinoba received the gift of the whole village of Mangroth. This meant the people were prepared to all their land for the benefit of all the villagers, not as individual bhoodan, but as community Gramdan (Gift of the Village). Vinoba received 23 lakh of land in Bihar, while walking from September 1952 to December 1954. Orissa, Tamil Nadu and Kerala contributed significantly to Gramdan. Vinoba firmly believed that, "We must establish the independent power of the people - this is to say, we must demonstrate a power opposed to the power of violence and other than the power to punish. The people are our God." Connected with Bhoodan and Gramdan, there were other programs. Important of these were Sampatti-Dan (Gift of the Wealth), Shramdan (Gift of the Labour), Shanti Sena (Army for Peace), Sarvodaya-Patra (the pot where every household gives daily handful of grain) and Jeevandan (Gift of Life). Jayaprakash Narayan in 1954 gave the gift of his life. Vinoba acknowledged it by giving the gift of his life.

Vinoba knew the strength of the padayatra (march on foot). He walked for 13 years throughout India. He had left Paunar on September 12, 1951 and returned on April 10, 1964. He started his Toofan Yatra (journey with the speed of high-velocity wind), using a vehicle, in Bihar in July 1965, which lasted for almost four years. He covered thousands of miles, addressed thousands of meetings and mobilized the people cutting the barriers of caste, class, language and religion. Some dacoits from the notorious Chambal Valley (a hideout of dacoits in the northern India) surrendered themselves to Vinoba in May 1960. For Vinoba, it was a victory of nonviolence.

On June 7, 1966, 50 years after his meeting with Gandhi, Vinoba announced that he was feeling a strong urge to free himself from outer visible activities and enter inward hidden form of spiritual action. After traveling through India, he returned to Paunar on November 2, 1969 and on October 7, 1970, he announced his decision to stay in one place. He observed a year of silence from

December 25, 1974 to December 25, 1975. In 1976, he undertook a fast to stop the slaughter of cows. His spiritual pursuits intensified as he withdrew from the activities.

After the death of Gandhiji, he went to what is now the state of Andhra Pradesh to work in an area where communists were inciting the landless peasants to kill the landlords and this work led to the Bhoodan or Land Gift movement when a landowner offered a hundred acres of land to the local harijan or untouchable community. From 1951 onwards he walked the length and breadth of India seeking land for the poor. As land alone was not enough, he developed the idea of Gramdan where villagers got together to pool their land and resources. A great deal has been written - often critical - about this effort to redistribute land but Moved by Love is not a political critique, it is an attempt to explain what motivated Vinoba and moved him to undertake the work he did. Although he said he did not want to be a guru, he never seemed to question the fact that decisions were often made simply on the basis of what he said, or that thousands of people just accepted his word because of who he was. On many occasions prominent politicians would come to pay their respects to him but then do little, if anything, about really implementing his ideas.

Vinoba also promoted the role of women after noting the patriarchal nature of India, both at a political and spiritual level, but his relationship with them was still that of an acharya (teacher), whether he liked it or not. He gives an account of why he set up six ashrams, including two that were to be run by women, acknowledging that they were run on his orders until he decided to stand back, after which there were to be no directors. Moved by Love also traces how Vinoba came to initiate the Shanti Sena or Peace Army which sought to bring communal harmony where before there was conflict, usually between Hindus and Moslems, and there is mention of his work in getting bandits - or dacoits - to give up their way of life with a good photo of one such well-known dacoit surrendering his arms to Vinoba. All the way through, however, Vinoba constantly refers to the Gita and other sacred scriptures as well as the teachings of those who inspired him - primarily Gandhi, the philosopher Shankara, and the Marathi poet-saint, Jnanadeva. When he was 75, he decided to adopt the Jain practice of becoming a Sthanakavasi or dweller in one place. There is no mention of the Emergency but it was in the same year that I met him at Paunar that he launched his campaign against cow slaughter, a decision which perplexed so many of his admirers, as it did not seem to relate to the overwhelming needs of the people of India at that time or respond to the issues being debated in the Sarvodaya Movement.

Vinoba Bhave died on 16th November, 1982 at the age of 87. He indeed done much for the upliftment of the socio-economic condition of the weaker sections of our society. A true Gandhian as he was, he was also a true friend of Harijans. He was the founder of the Bhoodan Movement through which he collected and donated land to the landless. Rich tributes were paid to him by one and all. Several leaders collected at the Paunar Ashram where he breathed his last.

Vinoba's contribution to the history of nonviolent movement remains significant. It has to be admitted, however, that the achievement of Bhoodan - Gramdan movement in the material terms was much below the expected target. According to an estimate in total 41,94,270 acres was obtained, and the land actual distributed according to 1975 statistics was 12,85,738 acres. 18,57,398 acres was found unfit for distribution. Some of the remaining land got entangled in legal hassles and some was deserved to be written off. As against it has to be noted that Vinoba's movement rekindled faith in non-violence and human values advocated by Gandhi. It presented an alternative to violence and a vision of non-violent society. It raised important questions regarding inequality prevalent in the society. Vinoba saw the land as the gift of God like air, water, sky and sunshine. He connected science with spirituality and the autonomous village with the world movement. He regarded the power of the people superior than power of the state. Many of his ideas remain relevant and inspiring in the strife-ridden modern times.

Vinoba sought nothing for himself, least of all recognition of his achievements. Rather, his has been a life selflessly devoted to finding and conveying the people an approach to the problem of poverty that is within the means of every man. He has given himself humbly and unstintingly in service to the people, mankind. He was awarded the first Ramon Magsaysay Award for Community Leadership, by the Government of Philippines recognizing his furtherance of the cause of arousing his countrymen toward voluntary action in relieving social injustice and economic inequalities.

Vinoba Bhave Cremated
Hindustan Times Correspondent

Paunar, Nov.16 – Amid cries of "*Vinoba amar rahe*" from the surging crowds, the mortal remains of Acharya Vinoba Bhave were consigned to the flames at 11.40 a.m. at the Gandhi Ghat today.

In a departure from the traditional Hindu practice, the funeral pyre was lit by Mahadevi, the adopted daughter of Vinoba as the late Acharya had wanted women to get a status equal with men. Ashramites said Vinoba was against women being relegated to the secondary status, and had desired that his last rites should be performed by women. The religious prayer that preceded the funeral were also led the women inmates of Paramdham Ashram.

Present on the occasion of the funeral were Prime Minister Indira Gandhi, Union Ministers R. Venkatraman, N.K.P. Salve, Vasant Sathe, Ghulam Nabi Azad, Maharashtra Chief Minister Baba Saheb Bhosale and his cabinet colleagues, State Governor, I.H. Latif, Karnataka Chief Minister Gundu Rao and a host of MLAs, MLCs and MPs.

Mrs. Gandhi arrived at the Paunar Ashram at 10.30 a.m. and was received by Union Minister of State for Shipping and Transport Sitaram Kesari shown present to receive her were Mr. Bhosale, Mr. Ramkrishna Bajaj and Vinoba's Secretary Bal Vijay Tembekar.

Exactly at 11 a.m. the funeral procession started. There was a lot jostling on the specially raised platform. The people were perched there dangerously on small rocks and were separated by small streams of water. Police had cordoned off the area, but people kept on breaking one barrier after another.

Later, lathi-wielding policemen were helpless onlookers as people hurried something or the other at the pyre. The Government respected the wishes of the Ashramites and did nothing against their wishes.

Hon'ble Prime Minister's Remarks on Vinoba Bhave during his visit to Vinoba Niketan, Trivandrum on September 3, 2005

Vinoba Bhave was one of the outstanding and truly exemplary followers of Mahatma Gandhi. He moulded himself in the image of the Mahatma and earned the loyalty of millions of our people in his lifetime. Vinobaji participated in the struggle for independence and suffered imprisonment. This year we celebrated the 75th anniversary of Dandi March. Mahatma Gandhi chose Vinobaji as one of the 78 persons to accompany him to Dandi to break the salt law. He was one of the earliest disciples of Gandhiji to have joined him at Sabarmati Ashram, right from its inception.

Gandhiji described Vinobaji as one of the "rare pearls" of the Sabarmati Ashram. As "one of those who have come not to be blessed but to bless, not to receive but to give." During 1939-40, when Second World War broke out, India was dragged into the war. Our nationalist leaders protested non-violently against the decision of the British Government. They expressed their opinion against war and spread the message of non-violence among people. The British Government imposed restrictions on freedom of speech and prevented the press from disseminating Gandhiji's message of non-violence. This encouraged Gandhiji to launch individual satyagraha solely for the cause of freedom of speech and expression. He chose Vinoba to lead that Satyagraha. Introducing Vinoba to rest of the country he explained the reason as to why he was selected. Gandhiji described him as a man who abolished every trace of untouchability from his heart. He praised him for his knowledge of Sanskrit and our scriptures and also for his deep understanding of Koran and Arabic. Vinobaji had also identified himself with the lowly and the lost, serving lepers and the poorest of the poor.

Vinobaji immersed himself in the Constructive Programme of Mahatma Gandhi. After Independence he became the Director of the Mahila Ashram in Wardha and later launched the historic Bhoodan Movement. Vinobaji recognized the needs of the poor for land and appealed to the higher sense of the landed rich. Many people were personally transformed by Vinobaji and responded to his appeal. Thousands of land owners parted with their land for the benefit of the landless poor. He made sure that at least a third of the land was donated to Dalits. His silent revolution to empower the landless was hailed by Bertrand Russell, the great philosopher and litterateur, as a "bloodless revolution".

Quotes of Vinoba

- "All revolutions are spiritual at the source. All my activities have the sole purpose of achieving a union of hearts."
- "Peace is something mental and spiritual. If there be peace in our (personal) life, it will affect the whole world"
- "Jai Jagat!—Victory to the world! "
- "It is a curious phenomena that God has made the hearts of the poor, rich and those of the rich, poor."
- "What we should aim at is the creation of people power, which is opposed to the power of violence and is different from the coercive power of state."
- "A country should be defended not by arms, but by ethical behavior."

References

- Publications Division, Acharya Vinoba Bhave, 1955, India.
- Shriman Narayan, Vinoba : His Life and Mission, 1970, Bombay.
- Suresh Ram, Vinoba Man and Message, 1961, Kashi.
- Prime Ministers Remarks on Vinoba on September 3, 2005 at Vinoba Niketan, Trivandrum.
- Raman Magsaysay Award Presentation Citation, 31 August, 1958, Manina Phillipines.

Bibliography

Bhave, Vinoba, Talks on Gita, Sarva Seva Sangh, Varanasi.

Bhave, Vinoba, The Essence of the Quran, Sarva Seva Sangh, Varanasi.

Bhave, Vinoba, Thoughts on Education, Sarva Seva Sangh, Varanasi.

Bhave, Vinoba, From Bhoodan to Gramdan, Sarvodaya Prachuralaya, Tanjore.

Bhave, Vinoba, Gramdan, Sarvodaya Prachuralaya, Tanjore.

Bhave, Vinoba, Gramdan : Why and How, Sarva Seva Sangh, Varanasi.

Bhave, Vinoba, Revolutionary Sarvodaya, Bharatiya Vidya Bhavan, Bombay.

Choudhary, M.M., Freedom for the Masses, Sarvodaya Prachuralaya, Tanjore.

Desai, Narayan, Shanti Sena in India, Sarva Seva Sangh, Varanasi.

Educational Reconstruction – 1937, Hindustani Talimi Sangh, Sevagram, Wardha.

Gandhi, M.K., India of My Dreams, Navajivan Publishing House, Ahmedabad.

Gramdan Movement : A Handbook, Planning Commission, New Delhi.

Kripalani, J.B. Sarvodaya and Democracy, Sarvodaya Prachuralaya, Tanjore.

Lanza, Del Vasto, Translated from French by Philip Leon, Gandhi to Vinoba, The New Pilgrimage, Rider and Company, London.

Misra B.R. V. for Vinoba – The Economics of the Bhoodan Movement, Orient Longmans.

Narayan, Jayaprakash, From Socialism to Sarvodaya, Sarva Seva Sangh, Varanasi.

Nargolkar, Vasant, The Creed of Saint Vinoba, Bhaatiya Vidya Bhavan, Bombay.

Prime Minister's Remarks at Vinoba Niketan, PMO.

Ram, Suresh, Vinoba and His Mission, Sarva Seva Sangh, Varanasi.

Sarva Seva Sangh, Planning for Sarvodaya, Varanasi.

Sharma, Jagdish Saran, Vinoba and Bhoodan – Bibliography, Indian National Congress, New Delhi.

Tandon, P.D. Vinoba Bhave – The Man and His Mission, Vora and Co. Publishers Ltd. 3, Round Building, Bombay 2.

Tennyson, Hallam, Saint on the March, published in India by W.D. Willis, Bombay.

Thackar, Vimala, The Philosophy of Land-Gift Mission, Sarvodaya Prachuralaya, Tanjore.

Thackar, Vimala, Vinoba Bhave on World Peace, Sarvodaya Prachuralaya, Tanjore.

Wilfred, Wellock, India's Social Revolution, Preston.

Glossary

Ahimsa	-	Non-violence
Akarma	-	Inaction
Ashram	-	Abode of a spiritual teacher
Bapu	-	Mahatma Gandhiji
Bhajan	-	A devotional song
Bhakti	-	Devotion
Bhoodan	-	Gift of land
Brahmachari	-	Celibate
Buddhi	-	Intelligence
Chakki	-	Grinding-stone
Chappal	-	Slipper
Charka	-	Spinning Wheel
Chitta	-	Mind

Crore	-	10 million
Dan	-	Giving of alms
Daman	-	Self control
Daya	-	Compassion
Deepak	-	Indigenous lamp with wicks
Deva	-	Bright God
Dharma	-	Sense of duty, Right conduct
Fakir	-	A mendicant, poor saint
Ganga	-	The sacred river Ganges in India
Ghee	-	Clarified Butter
Gita	-	Bhagavad Gita
Gramdan	-	Gift of the whole village land
Gramraj	-	Village self-government
Gram Sabha	-	Village Council
Grama Seva Mandal	-	Village Service Association
Guru	-	Master, Preceptor
Gyan	-	Knowledge
Karma	-	Outward action
Khadi	-	Hand-spun and hand-woven cloth
Kranti	-	Revolution
Kriya	-	Activity
Lakh	-	100,000
Lok-Shakti	-	Power of People
Lota	-	A small jug for taking water

Mela	-	Fair
Moksha	-	Emancipation
Mukti	-	Salvation
Nai Talim	-	Basic Education
Namaz	-	Prayer at a Mosque
Padayatra	-	Journey on foot
Prajapati	-	The Creator
Rajas	-	The quality of passion
Ram Rajya	-	Rule of God
Rishi	-	A seer, sage
Sammelan	-	Conference
Sandhya	-	Prayer or oblation to the Sun
Satya	-	Truth
Satyagraha	-	Adherence to truth
Satyagrahi	-	One who offers Satyagraha
Seva	-	Service
Shanti	-	Peace
Shanti Sena	-	Peace Brigade
Shastras	-	Hindu Scriptures
Shramdan	-	Gift of physical labour
Swadeshi	-	Exclusive use of articles made in one's own country
Takli	-	A small spindle for hand-spinning
Tamas	-	Inertia, darkness
Tapas	-	Practicing austerity

Thali	-	A metal plate used for taking food
Upanishads	-	Ancient *sanskrit* books propounding Vedanta Philosophy
Vande Mataram	-	Salutation to Mother India
Vinoba Kuti	-	A cottage in Sabarmati Ashram
Yagya	-	Offering or sacrifice
Yamaraj	-	The God of Death
Yoga	-	The art of spiritual living

Index

Index

❑ ❑ ❑